CULTURE SMART!
NEPAL

Tessa Feller

·K·U·P·E·R·A·R·D·

First published in Great Britain 2008
by Kuperard, an imprint of Bravo Ltd
59 Hutton Grove, London N12 8DS
Tel: +44 (0) 20 8446 2440   Fax: +44 (0) 20 8446 2441
www.culturesmartguides.com
Inquiries: sales@kuperard.co.uk

Culture Smart! is a registered trademark of Bravo Ltd

Distributed in the United States and Canada
by Random House Distribution Services
1745 Broadway, New York, NY 10019
Tel: +1 (212) 572-2844   Fax: +1 (212) 572-4961
Inquiries: csorders@randomhouse.com

Series Editor Geoffrey Chesler
Design Bobby Birchall

ISBN 978 1 85733 458 6

British Library Cataloguing in Publication Data
A CIP catalogue entry for this book is available from the
British Library

Printed in Malaysia

This book is available for special discounts for bulk purchases
for sales promotions or premiums. Special editions, including
personalized covers, excerpts of existing books, and corporate
imprints, can be created in large quantities for special needs.

For more information in the USA write to Special
Markets/Premium Sales, 1745 Broadway, MD 6–2, New York,
NY 10019, or e-mail specialmarkets@randomhouse.com.

In the United Kingdom contact Kuperard publishers at the
address at the top of the page.

Cover image: Stupa and prayer flags at Bodhnath. *Travel Ink/David Guyler*

Images on pages 14, 16, 20, 38, 39, 50, 52, 53, 66, 95, 97, 100, 101, 106, 108, 130,
132, and 142 courtesy of Stefan Feller.

Images on the following pages reproduced under Creative Commons License
Attribution 2.5: 19 © santoshkc; 26 © Yves Picq; 44 © Pavel Novak; 71 © Steve Evans;
74 © Andy Carvin; 77 © Wen-Yan King; 93 and 145 © McKay Savage; 104, 112, 118,
119, 124, 125, 135, and 158 © Sigismund von Dobschütz; 121 © Kogo; 123 © Wolfgang
Beyer; 127 © Bryan nys; 134 © Prince Roy; and 143 © Rainer Hessner.
Page 68 © iStockphoto

About the Author

TESSA FELLER studied German and Spanish at Edinburgh University before training as a teacher and translator. She has worked in several countries, including Austria, Russia, and Germany, where she is now based. She lived in Nepal from 2002 to 2004, when her husband was posted there with the German Development Service (Deutscher Entwicklungsdienst). Her youngest son was born in Kathmandu.

contents

contents

Map of Nepal

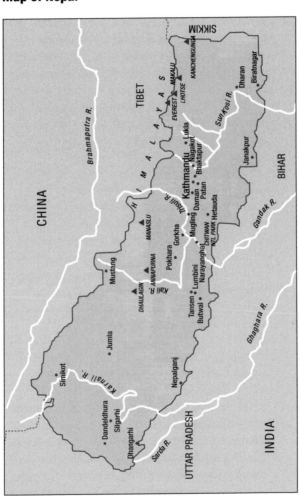

introduction

In the popular imagination, Nepal is a land of eternal snow, where heroic mountaineers and Sherpas valiantly plant flags on the roof of the world, or perish in the attempt. And yet there is far more to Nepal than the ultimate challenge to mountaineers. It has to be one of the most diverse countries in the world, for its climate, scenery, flora, fauna, and not least on account of the complex variety of its cultural, ethnic, and religious weave.

Contrasts and incongruities abound: spectacular snowcapped peaks rise above dusty plains; the Abominable Snowman meets abominable heat; two-, three-, and four-wheeled vehicles careen chaotically around an overcrowded capital, while in the mountains, nothing moves faster than a mule. The beauty of Nepal's people, landscape, and vegetation stands out against a background of dust, dirt, and urban ugliness. There are many divisions—between rich and poor, urban and rural, highlands and lowlands, privileged and penniless, high caste and untouchable, and—recently—king and country. And yet a certain "unity in diversity" binds the country together.

Never a colony, Nepal was isolated from the rest of the world for centuries. Its extreme terrain has both protected it from outside influence and slowed its development. Its relative inaccessibility has allowed pockets of contrasting cultures to flourish. At the same time, these have largely coexisted in peace, thanks to a tolerance, openness, and mutual respect that prevail by and large to this day.

The country has been torn apart over the last decade by civil war, and thrown into despair by the loss of its royal family in 2001. And still the people you meet remain stoic, fatalist, accepting what befalls them. They continue to rise and retire with the sun. Agricultural rhythms dictate the pace of life. The suffering caused by civil strife may be great, but it is not something they wish to bother visitors with.

Culture Smart! Nepal introduces you to the cultural, ethnic, and religious mosaic that is Nepal. It seeks to explain the complexities of all aspects of Nepalese life, from the home, to the marketplace, to the office. It describes how the country's geography and history have helped shape contemporary society, and how religion defines social structures and leaves its indelible imprint on the Nepalese mentality. It helps you to understand Nepalese attitudes and values, giving you an idea of what to expect, and how to avoid *faux pas.*

You are unlikely to meet an unfriendly face in Nepal. It may be one of the ten poorest countries in the world, but you will always be made welcome. Whatever the reason for your visit, understanding the cultural backdrop will help you get beyond the friendly smiles and greetings, making it an extremely enlightening and rewarding experience. *Namaste*!

Key Facts

Official Name	State of Nepal (since 2006)	Previously: Kingdom of Nepal
Capital City	Kathmandu	Pop. of Kathmandu valley (cities of Kathmandu, Patan, and Bhaktapur): c. 1 million
Main Cities	Pokhara	Pop. c. 200,000
Area	56,827 square miles (147,181 sq. km)	Officially, Nepal uses the metric system. In practice, both metric and imperial are used.
Geography	Landlocked, between Tibet/China to the north and India to the south	On a latitude with the Sahara Desert/Florida (28 00 N, 84 00 E)
Terrain	Rugged Himalayas in north, central hill region, flat river plains in south	
Land Use	Arable land 16.07%. Permanent crops, 0.85%: other, 83.08%	Most Nepalese are subsistence farmers. Best agricultural land is on southern plains
Climate	Alpine climate in high mountains, temperate central valleys, subtropical southern plains	
Population	28,901,790 (est. July 2007)	
Life Expectancy	60.78 for men; 60.33 for women	
Age Structure	0–14 yrs: 38.3%; 15–64 yrs: 57.9%; 65 yrs and over: 3.8%	

Literacy	48.6%: 62.7% men, 34.9% women	
Ethnic Make-up	*Chhetri* 15.5%, *Bahun* 12.5%, Magar 7%, Tharu 6.6%, Tamang 5.5%, Newar 5.4%, Muslim 4.2%, Kami 3.9%, Yadav 3.9%, other 35.5%	
Languages	Nepali 47.8%, Maithili 12.1%, Bhojpuri 7.4%, Tharu 5.8%, Tamang 5.1%, Newar 3.6%, Magar 3.3%, Awadhi 2.4%, other 12.5%	
Religion	Hindu 80.6%, Buddhist 10.7%, Muslim 4.2%, other 4.5%	
Currency	Nepali Rupee (NPR) (100 paisa). 1 lakh = 100,000 rupees	Pegged to the Indian rupee. In November 2007, US $1 = NPR 63.89
Government	Parliamentary democracy. Until 2006, a constitutional Hindu monarchy. Now secular, and declared a republic in 2007, a new constitution is to be prepared.	
Media	*Gorkhapatra* and *Kantipur* are Nepalese-language dailies; *Budhabar* and *Deshantar* are weeklies.	There are currently two state TV channels and six private channels.
Media: English Language	*The Kathmandu Post*, *The Himalayan Times*, and *The Rising Nepal* are English dailies.	*The Nepali Times* is a weekly. Some international periodicals available in Kathmandu
Electricity	220 volts, 50 Hz	Usually three-round-prong plugs. Power supply erratic
Video/TV	PAL system	
Telephone	Nepal's country code is 977.	To dial out: 00 plus country code
Time	GMT + 5 ¾ hours	EST + 10 ¾ hours

chapter one

LAND &
PEOPLE

GEOGRAPHY

Sandwiched between China to the north, and India to the south, Nepal runs approximately 500 miles (800 km) from northwest to southeast, and is between 56 and 143 miles wide (90 and 230 km), covering an area of 56,827 square miles (147,181 sq. km). It is home not only to Mount Everest, at 29,029 feet (8,848 m) the world's highest mountain, but to eight of the world's ten highest peaks, and several hundred more exceeding 20,000 feet (6,000 m).

The Himalayas give the country its unique appeal to the outside world, but this picture can be misleading: altitudes descend to less than 200 feet (60 m), and more than 40 percent of the land area is below 3,300 feet (1,000 m). The extreme variation in altitude within a small space influences everything, from Nepal's climate to its ethnicity and demography, history, and political and economic development.

More than 60 million years ago, the Indo-Australian tectonic plate collided with the Eurasian continent. The resultant crunching of the Earth's crust over millennia has created a series of mountain systems running in a northwest/southeast direction. These divide Nepal into roughly parallel strips of different ecological character.

The Ganges plains extend some 25 miles (40 km) into Nepal along its southern border with India, forming the lowlands or Terai, and rising to a maximum 1,000 feet (300 m) above sea level. This area was infested with malaria and largely uninhabitable until sprayed with DDT in the 1950s. Now its dense forests have been cleared to make room for people from the hills, and its fertile plains, though just a fifth of the territory, house a good 50 percent of the total population.

Separated from the Terai by the Mahabharat range of hills are the *pahar* (mid-hills), covering 60 percent of the land area and ranging from 1,000 feet (300 m) to nearly 15,000 feet (4,500 m) in altitude. Characteristic of these are flat, enclosed high valleys that have been inhabited for centuries, such as the highly populous and cultivated Kathmandu valley and Pokhara.

North of the mid-hills is the great Himalaya, which covers almost a fifth of the nation's territory. The few treacherous paths that traverse these high mountains, formerly trade routes between Tibet and India, are now mainly used by backpackers. The sparsely populated inner valleys of the Himalaya are screened to an extent from wind and rain, but can only be reached on foot or by airplane.

The Transhimalaya beyond is an arid desert region along the Tibetan border, in the rain shadow of the Himalayas at an average altitude of 19,700 feet (6,000 m) above sea level.

CLIMATE

There are effectively two seasons in Nepal: the dry season from October to the end of May, and the monsoon, which starts in June and goes on until

the end of September. The best times to visit are after the monsoon, in October and November, when the country is lush green and the air is clearest, and February (when the rhododendron forests are in full bloom in the countryside) through to April, before it becomes too sultry.

The Himalayas form a meteorological divide, separating the moist monsoon climate of southern Asia on one side from the arid continental climate of the Tibetan steppes on the other. The monsoon arrives from the southeast, and falls most heavily on the southern and southeastern slopes of the mountains. This is not a good time to travel, as the mountains are often obscured by clouds, and road conditions can be very poor.

Average annual precipitation is approximately 98 inches (2,500 mm) in the east of Nepal, and 148 inches (3,755 mm) in Pokhara. Compare this with 140 inches (3,552 mm) in Seathwaite, the wettest inhabited place in England. The difference is that precipitation in England is spread evenly over twelve months, whereas in Nepal, it is concentrated into two. Rivers you can paddle in one day can turn into raging torrents overnight, sometimes washing away whole villages, roads, and bridges.

Temperature and climate are determined by the country's position in the northern hemisphere (it is on a latitude with the Central Saharan desert) and by altitude. While temperatures in the high mountains are permanently below freezing, temperatures in the Terai may reach 104°F (40°C) in the hottest months (May and June before the monsoon breaks). These temperatures are compounded by high humidity. Temperatures in the capital regularly rise to 86°F (30°C) in summer, but drop pleasantly at night due to its altitude (4,265 ft/1,300 m above sea level). In January, temperatures in Kathmandu may reach 68°F (20°C) in the sun, but fall to near freezing point at night. Pokhara and especially the Terai are significantly warmer, although the Terai can feel very cold in January because blanket fog sometimes fails to rise for days at a time.

Broadly speaking, the Terai enjoys a tropical climate, the mid-hills are tropical to temperate, and the high mountains have an alpine climate. Hillsides are terraced and cultivated up to 8,900 feet (2,700 m) or the level of the clouds and mist on their southern slopes. Barley and potatoes grow to an altitude of 14,100 feet (4,300 m), which is also the tree line. The snow line begins at about 16,400 feet (5,000 m), much higher than in the Alps.

THE PEOPLE

Nepal has a population of approximately 29 million people, growing fast at an annual rate of 2.3 percent. There can be few geographical areas of similar size in this world as ethnically diverse: the census of 2001 identified ninety-two living languages, and a hundred-and-three distinct caste and ethnic groups.

Several waves of migration over two millennia brought Indo-Aryan peoples from the south together with Tibeto-Burmese peoples from the north. The country's sheer topography and climatic peculiarities facilitated the preservation of separate cultural enclaves.

A demographic map of the country roughly reflects the high mountain, mid-hill, and lowland zones described in the section on geography. Each zone can be further divided from east to west, with different ethnic groups inhabiting different regions.

In the high Himalayas, Buddhist peoples of Tibetan descent predominate. These include the Sherpas in the northeast, Tamang in the Central Himalayas and hills, and Thakali further west. The *pahar* (mid-hills) region is home to Rai and Limbu peoples in the east, Newars around the Kathmandu valley, and Gurung and Magar further west, as well as the originally Gorkha caste-structured Hindu Parbatiya, who include the two highest castes, *Bahuns* and *Chhetris*, and *dalits* (untouchables). Today the Parbatiya make up 40.3 percent of the total population.

Until the eradication of malaria in the 1950s, the Tharu people were almost the sole inhabitants of the Terai region. Nowadays it is home to migrants from the hill areas and population overflow from the Ganges plains in India. Dominant ethnic groups are the Maithili in the east, Bhojpuri in the central Terai, and Abadhi in the west. Large

numbers of Muslims from India have also settled
in the Terai. Approximately 7.3 percent of the
population currently lives in the mountains,
44.3 percent live in the central mid-hill region,
and 48.4 percent now live in the Terai. These
regions comprise 35 percent, 42 percent, and
23 percent of the total land area respectively.

A BRIEF HISTORY

There are two problems with historical accounts
of Nepal. One is that most are in fact restricted to
the story of the Kathmandu valley. The second is
that the country's history is inevitably recounted
from the point of view of the dominant higher-
caste Hindus (*Bahuns* and *Chhetris*). This in itself,
however, is a reflection of the country's history:
the Kathmandu valley and higher-caste Hindu
groups who live there have dominated politics,
the economy, and Nepali society for centuries. At
the same time, other religious and ethnic groups,
although subordinated in the Hindu order of
things, have traditionally been tolerated. Indeed,
the country's relative isolation has made it a safe
haven for those escaping domination elsewhere.

Early Inhabitants

Excavations have shown that the Kathmandu
valley has been inhabited for at least 9,000 years.
Both Indo-Aryan migrants from the south and

Tibeto-Burmese groups from the north are believed to have been present in the valley since about 1000 BCE.

The ancient Indian epics, the *Mahabharata* and *Ramayana*, provide the first documented references to the Kiratis, a Mongoloid people who dominated the valley for almost a millennium from around the eighth century BCE. The Rai and Limbu peoples of eastern Nepal are believed to be their descendants.

Several flourishing Hindu kingdoms in the Terai in the first millennium BCE included that of the Shakya dynasty, whose most famous prince was Siddhārtha Gautama Buddha, born around 563 BCE in Lumbini. He later renounced his rank to lead an ascetic life and become the founder of the Buddhist faith.

The Licchavis, 450–879

The Licchavis were Indo-Aryans who invaded from northern India around 300 CE, coming to

power in the middle of the fifth century. They introduced the Hindu caste system that continues to divide society to this day, but also set a precedent for religious tolerance and syncretism. The first Licchavi king, Manadeva I, is said to have worshipped at both Hindu and Buddhist shrines.

This was a period of great economic prosperity and cultural activity. The Buddhist temple

complexes of Swayambunath and Bodhnath date from the Licchavi era, as do the Hindu temples of Changu Narayan and Pashupatinath. Mountain paths that still exist today became important trade routes linking Tibet with India. During this time, Buddhism found its way to Tibet, and the pagoda style typical of Licchavi architecture was adopted in China and Japan.

The Thakuri Kings, 602–1200

The Thakuri kings reigned from the seventh to the thirteenth centuries, cementing their relationships with north and south by means of strategic marriages. The daughter of Amsuvarman, the first Thakuri king, married a Tibetan prince and is said to have converted her husband to Buddhism. She is still honored today as a reincarnation of the Green Tara goddess of Tibetan Buddhism. The city of Kathmandu also dates from this era, having been founded in the tenth century. Meanwhile, the advance of Muslim conquerors in the south appears to have caused both Buddhist and Hindu clerics to take refuge in the Kathmandu valley.

The Malla Dynasty, 1200–1768

The Malla kings were a Newar dynasty that reigned in the Kathmandu valley from 1200 to 1768. The Newars today consider themselves to be the original inhabitants of the valley, but no one really knows where they came from.

After more than a century of feudal conflict, and a devastating invasion by Muslim Mughals in 1349, King Jayasthiti Malla succeeded in uniting the whole valley in 1382. He sought to impose order by implementing the rules of orthodox Hinduism. The caste system was extended to include the Buddhist Newars.

Buddhist priests took the highest social rank, like their Hindu (*Bahun*) counterparts, followed by noblemen, officials, shopkeepers, and farmers. Monks were permitted to marry and the status of priests also became hereditary, thus reinforcing their status within the social hierarchy. Priests began to perform more worldly jobs and carry out their priestly duties as secondary occupations. The tantric form of Buddhism began to spread (see Chapter 3). Newar, a Tibeto-Burmese language distinct from Tibetan and Nepali, became the language of state.

King Yaksha Malla, grandson of Jayasthiti, pursued an expansionist policy until the country extended from the Ganges in the south to Tibet in the north, and from the Kali Gandaki River in the west to Sikkim. On his death in 1482, the kingdom split into three rival kingdoms ruled from Bhaktapur, Kathmandu, and Patan. Political feuding continued for the next two centuries, eventually inviting disaster, but culturally this period was a golden age, in which the three kingdoms vied to outdo each other in terms of architecture and art. Many of the buildings and works of art still to be admired today in Bhaktapur, Patan, and Kathmandu date from this era.

The Shah Kings and the Unification of Nepal, 1768–1846

The Hindu rulers of the Shah dynasty from the tiny kingdom of Gorkha, some 62 miles (100 km) to the west, had meanwhile been growing in strength. Although both Muslim and British troops rushed to help the Mallas, King Prithvi Narayan Shah of Gorkha was able to defeat them and unify Nepal in 1768.

Fearing European intervention, the new ruler expelled all Christian missionaries from the country and refused entry to foreigners. Nepal entered a (first) period of self-imposed isolation—in retrospect perhaps a blessing, as the country was to be spared ever being ruled by foreigners.

In their thirst for new land, the Shah kings spread throughout the mid-hills of Nepal, taking with them both their religion and their Nepali language, a language of Indo-Aryan origin. For a while the country extended from Kashmir in the west to Sikkim in the east. The Chinese put a stop to their expansion when they attempted to conquer Tibet.

War Against the British
Meanwhile the influence of the British on the Indian subcontinent was growing. In 1814, a border dispute with the British East India Company led to war.

Significantly, although defeated, Nepal was never actually colonized. By the Treaty of Sugauli of 1816, the Nepalese were forced to give up Sikkim and much of the Terai to Britain, and tolerate a British resident in Kathmandu, stationed there to monitor the situation. This established the country's present-day borders. A further long period of isolation began. The British residents were to be the only foreigners allowed into the country for more than a century.

THE GURKHAS

The British were so impressed by the valor and tenacity of these hardy mountain warriors, that they not only allowed them to surrender honorably with their arms, but began to employ them in the ranks of the East India Company's army. When they later proved their loyalty during the Indian Mutiny of 1857, the British Army created its elite Gurkha regiments. Since then they have become one of Nepal's most famous exports, serving not only in the British but also in the Indian Army and as mercenaries elsewhere. Their courage is legendary, and Gurkhas have served in the British Army in both world wars, the Falklands, and Iraq. In return for their help during the two world wars, Nepal was assured of its independence and guaranteed duty-free transit of commodities through India.

The Ranas, 1846–1951

In 1846, Jung Bahadur Rana, a nephew of the king, had many of the most important people in the country massacred in the Kot courtyard next to Kathmandu's Durbar Square, before declaring himself prime minister. Thereafter power was in the hands of the Rana family, who became hereditary prime ministers. The Shahs were relegated to the role of puppet kings with little more than a ceremonial function. The Ranas maintained cordial relations with Britain, rushing to help the British during the Indian Mutiny in 1857 with 8,000 Gurkhas, although the country remained isolated from the outside world.

The Hinduization of Nepal

The dominance of the Hindu ruling elite became firmly established during the Shah and Rana eras. Having unified Nepal, the ruling Parbatiya Hindus needed to consolidate their political control. They also wanted to raise revenue quickly from the conquered kingdoms in order to be able to continue expansion. Officers were rewarded with *jagirs*—gifts of conquered land.

At the same time, peace had priority over conformity. The complete subordination of so many tiny kingdoms of such varied ethnic and religious backgrounds would have been difficult. The caste system, officially codified for the first time in Jung Bahadur Rana's *Muluki Ain* (civil code) of 1854, was to give them the legal and social structure they needed to integrate the many different ethnic communities into a coherent unit.

By prescribing caste status for all groups according to how closely they adhered to Hindu norms, the code put pressure on non-Hindus to conform to Hindu standards. Groups that

consumed alcohol or pork were for example lower caste than most high-caste Hindus. The *Muluki Ain* also dealt with subjects as varied as land tenure, inheritance, marriage, and sexual relations. It banned certain practices, such as the consumption of beef. It established the Hindu culture and way of thinking as the basis of the state and law, although it was neutral on the subject of other religions.

Different ethnic groups responded in different ways to Hindu dominance. Some, such as the Magars and Thakalis, sought to integrate and adopted Hindu customs. Others resisted. Many Limbus thus left for Sikkim and Darjeeling. The remoteness of other communities, such as the Sherpas, allowed them to ignore what was going on elsewhere. The recruitment of large numbers of soldiers from different ethnic groups into the British and Indian armies helped spread Parbatiya culture, however, as Nepali became the common language within the Gurkha regiments. It can be said that while the Tibeto-Burmese peoples have given the country its cultural diversity, the Indo-Aryans provide the links that hold the country together.

Other significant reforms introduced during the Ranas' rule included the banning of the practice of *suttee* (burning widows on their husbands' funeral pyres), and the abolition of slavery in 1924.

The Beginnings of Democracy

India's independence in 1947 and the Chinese annexation of Tibet in 1951 meant that Nepal became a buffer zone between the two powers. The success of India's independence movement led to calls within Nepal to end the autocratic rule of the Ranas. In 1947, the Nepali National Congress was established as the first people's representative body. Known after 1950 as the Nepali Congress Party, it was increasingly supported by many Nepalis, including members of the royal family, and by India, which feared weak Rana rule.

In 1950, King Tribhuvan was forced to flee to India because of his support for the Nepali National Congress. His infant son was briefly proclaimed king by the Ranas, a move that provoked a short civil war. Tribhuvan returned to Kathmandu in 1951 with the support of Nehru to set up a new government under a non-Rana prime minister. King Mahendra succeeded his father in

1955, and in 1959 Nepal held its first general election. By December 1960, however, the king had declared the failure of democracy. He returned to an authoritarian style of government, banning political parties and introducing the party-less Panchayat system of government.

The Panchayat System, 1962–90
To all appearances, the Panchayat system introduced in 1962 allowed people to choose their own representatives. It involved a pyramid-like structure of Panchayat (councils) elected at the local level. Local councils then elected representatives for district councils, which in turn appointed representatives to parliament. At the top of the pyramid sat the king, however, who retained absolute authority over the prime minister and parliament. The royal family thus maintained its control of politics and the economy, while the army and police were given a free hand to suppress dissent. The media were strictly censored, and many of the leaders of the Nepali Congress Party spent extended periods in jail during this time. Corruption was rife, and although it is impossible to prove, much of both government spending and foreign aid evaporated long before it reached the grass roots.

There were some achievements. Government programs built schools, increased literacy, and sought to improve communications as a means of development. Roads were built, especially with Indian investment. In an effort to develop one common culture, the Panchayat promoted Nepali as the national language and sole language of education. This policy further consolidated the dominance of the high-caste, Nepali-speaking elite, putting ethnic minorities at a disadvantage.

King Birendra and the Constitutional Monarchy, 1990–2001

In 1979, riots erupted in Kathmandu to protest the slow pace of development and perceived corruption. King Birendra, who had taken over on the death of his father, Mahendra, in 1972, offered his people the choice between a reformed Panchayat and a multiparty system. The Panchayat won by a narrow margin, and thus survived for a further decade. However, support for a multiparty system was growing, and increasing democratization was the consequence.

In 1989 an Indian blockade exacerbated a difficult economic situation in the country. The Nepali Congress called a mass demonstration in February 1990, demanding an end to the Panchayat and Indian dominance. The arrests of its leaders were followed by general strikes and further protests, which were initially suppressed brutally. The king preempted an escalation of the violence, however, by announcing the dissolution of the Panchayat and introducing a multiparty system. A new constitution emphasized the sovereignty of the people and established adult franchise, a two-house parliamentary system, a constitutional monarchy, multiparty democracy, and an independent judiciary. In May 1991, free elections were held.

Once in power, the leaders of the people's movement did not have a coherent agenda, and the first decade of democracy was characterized by political instability. Democracy brought a degree of political awareness, but few economic or social changes. The definition of the Hindu state was retained. The constitution of 1990 emphasized people's participation, but did not include provisions for local government. This led to a centralized structure and left a huge gulf between urban Nepal and the hill districts.

The Maoist Insurgency, 1996–2006

Various Communist groups participated actively in the people's movement of 1989–90. The Communist Party of Nepal (United Marxist-Leninist) became the second-biggest political party in the elections of 1991, and remains a mainstream political party representing the left. The CPN (Maoist) is a breakaway group formed in 1995 after numerous splits in the movement. It has never been satisfied with the constitutional monarchy and demands the creation of a people's republic.

Disenchanted with the constant political infighting, the CPN denounced the other Communist groups for participating in the parliamentary process in 1994, and launched a People's War in 1996, with attacks on police stations in the western and mid-western regions. Brutal and indiscriminate police retaliation resulted in the almost complete alienation of the rural population. By 2001 at least forty-five out of a total of seventy-five districts were classified as "highly affected" by the insurgency.

THE ROYAL MASSACRE

On June 1, 2001, ten members of the royal family were shot dead in the royal palace. A stunned Nepali public refused to believe the official story, that in a drug-crazed frenzy, after being refused permission to marry the woman of his choice, Crown Prince Dipendra had killed nine of his closest relatives before turning the gun on himself. Rumors still abound as to the real nature of the event, ranging from a Maoist plot, to an attempted coup by foreign intelligence agencies, to a conspiracy organized by the new king.

When a brief cease-fire in July 2001 permitted talks, the Maoists took the opportunity to demand a new constitution, arguing that after the massacre, "the traditional monarchy based on feudal nationalism has ended."

On November 26, 2001, the government responded to the resumption of Maoist attacks on police and military installations in the western hills by declaring a state of emergency and mobilizing the army against them for the first time. Taking advantage of the post-9/11 world political climate, they also declared the Maoists to be terrorists. Whereas the first six years of the civil war had cost three thousand lives, an estimated seven thousand people were killed in the first year of the army's involvement. Human rights abuses abounded on both sides.

By late 2002 the insurgents controlled seven of seventy-five districts, mainly in the mid-west. In these areas, they set up people's governments and courts, levied taxes, organized development programs, and controlled basic health and education services. They then began to use terror to expand into other areas, murdering or threatening local leaders to send them into flight to create power vacuums, blocking roads and bridges to isolate regions, forcibly recruiting, and generally intimidating the population. Rural people were often caught in a no-win situation, coerced into feeding the Maoists by night, and punished for doing so by the Royal Nepal Army by day.

As it seemed unlikely in May 2002 that Prime Minister Deuba's government would obtain the majority it needed to extend the state of emergency, he asked King Gyanendra to dissolve the House of Representatives and call elections. In order to prevent the Maoists influencing the elections through intimidation, Deuba then simply replaced existing, elected local committees with government officials. Democratic structures were thus removed at both national and local levels.

When it then appeared that it would be impossible to organize any elections for as long as the Maoist conflict lasted, Deuba asked the king to postpone them indefinitely. Gyanendra seized the opportunity to restore the absolute power of the monarchy. He dismissed the government on October 4, 2002, and proceeded to appoint a series of governments himself. Their mandate was to end the insurgency and organize parliamentary elections. This was made impossible by the Maoists, and by the Royal Nepal Army, who refused to take orders from anyone but the king.

The Royal Putsch of February 2005

Citing the continued political disarray and inability of the political parties to contain the insurgency, Gyanendra sacked the government again on February 1, 2005, declared a state of emergency, and assumed direct rule himself. It amounted to a royal putsch, not because he had dissolved parliament, given that the latter was illegitimate anyway, but because at the same time he suspended many fundamental human rights. Many politicians,

journalists, human rights activists, students, and intellectuals were arrested, and the state assumed control over all media. Immediately after the broadcasting of Gyanendra's "putsch speech" on February 1, all telecommunication systems were switched off. The country was cut off from the outside world.

But the king had miscalculated. By depriving people of their fundamental rights, he only made the political parties and civil society into opponents of the monarchy. His actions finally caused the Maoist rebels and political parties to unite against him. Pro-democracy demonstrations became increasingly anti-monarchy.

Despite day-time curfews, demonstration bans, and violent clampdowns by the security forces, a nineteen-day protest organized by the seven-party alliance and civil society with the tacit support of the Maoists in April 2006 drew unprecedented numbers of demonstrators representing all sectors of society throughout the country. On April 24 the king backed down and reinstated the parliament he had dissolved in 2002.

A parliamentary resolution stripped the king of his powers and privileges, established an interim government, and officially secularized what had been the only Hindu state in the world. On November 21, 2006, a declaration of peace ended the ten-year insurgency that, according to UN figures, had left thirteen thousand people dead, and one hundred thousand displaced.

NEPAL TODAY

Administratively Nepal's seventy-five districts are subdivided into around four thousand Village Development Committees (VDCs), and sixty municipalities, which are generally communities of over twenty thousand inhabitants. The VDCs and municipalities are further divided into wards, the number of which depends on the population.

Democracy has not yet worked for Nepal. The judiciary, consisting of a Supreme Court, sixteen appeal courts, and seventy-five district courts, has a reputation for being far from independent. Since 2002 there have been no elected bodies at local level. A climate of fear means people are afraid to stand for

office in many areas. The political parties are not democratic in themselves. Even the Maoist leadership is predominantly high-caste Hindu.

Since unification in 1768, Nepal has been multiethnic, multilingual, multicultural, and multireligious. Nevertheless, discrimination and exclusion have always been features, and only a small minority have profited from development. Exposure to education and democracy, however, has brought the interests of underprivileged groups increasingly to the fore. Ethnic unrest has erupted in the Terai because the Madhesi feel that the hill-dominated elites, now including the Maoists, are denying them a fair share in power. They would like greater autonomy for the Terai.

The Maoists joined the interim government in January 2007. For a while, all were agreed that a constituent assembly should decide the country's future. In September 2007, however, the Maoists withdrew from government, demanding the immediate declaration of a republic before a democratic vote. On December 24, 2007, the government agreed to the abolition of the monarchy and the declaration of a "federal, democratic, republican state," to be approved by the yet-to-be-elected constitutional assembly. The king was allowed to remain in his palace until then. People thus began talking of a "paper republic," and to lose faith not only in the king, but in all political institutions.

At the time of writing, constituent assembly elections have been rescheduled for April 2008. It is by no means certain that they will be held, or that a political force capable of uniting the country will emerge. Traditionalists argue that, for all its faults, the monarchy was at least an institution with which almost all population groups could identify. There is no other obvious icon capable of uniting so many different groups. The gulf between urban and rural areas remains, as does the country's most persistent problem: poverty.

Nepal remains one of the ten poorest countries in the world—37.7 percent of the population live on less than US $1 per day. Of a thousand children, seventy-four do not live to see their fifth birthday. Only 35 percent of the population has access to adequate sanitation facilities.

Secularization and parliament's recent declaration of an end to discrimination against untouchables represent important reforms, but they will mean little unless there is a fundamental change in the thinking of the high-caste elite to allow fair participation of all groups.

THE ECONOMY

Kathmandu's urban anthill is not "the real Nepal." In fact the urban population represents just 9 percent of the total, a statistic that reflects the rural nature of the country. Although it accounts for just 38 percent of GDP, agriculture provides three-quarters of all Nepalis with a livelihood.

Most are subsistence farmers, eking out an existence on the cultivable 20 percent of the land

area. Farmers in the Terai typically work little more than 2.5 acres (1 hectare) of land, may have a water buffalo and a cow to provide milk, and will give 50 percent of their harvest to the landowner. The Terai generally produces an agricultural surplus, some of which is redistributed to cover food deficiencies in other areas. The main crops are rice, maize, wheat, lentils, millet, and potatoes.

Population pressure and the Maoist conflict have led to migration from the countryside to the towns, and from the hill regions to the Terai, but development in industry is not sufficient to provide jobs for all. Industry accounts for about 20 percent of GDP, but employs just 6 percent of the population. There is a severe shortage of skilled labor, further exacerbated by workers fleeing poverty and/or conflict to try their luck abroad, mainly in India, the Gulf states, and Malaysia. Nepal's largest source of foreign currency, more than it receives from exports, aid, and tourism put together, comes in the form of remittances from people working abroad.

Tourism is the country's most important industry, although it has suffered as a result of the Maoist conflict. Traditional cottage industries feed the tourist industry with handicrafts.

The manufacturing industries are concentrated in the Kathmandu valley and the Terai. In the absence of natural resources of any significance, they are mainly concerned with processing imported raw materials, or with the processing of agricultural produce such as grain, jute, tobacco, and sugar cane. There are also cement and brick factories, soft drinks plants (American investors), and chemical

factories (Indian investors). The main exports are vegetable ghee, clothing, carpets, leather goods, jute goods, and grain. More than half of all exports go to India. The USA (garments) and Germany (carpets) are its second- and third-biggest export partners.

Foreign aid finances more than 60 percent of development and around one-quarter of Nepal's annual budget of approximately US $1.4 billion. It is equal to more than 10 percent of the GDP.

VALUES &
ATTITUDES

It is difficult to generalize about values and
attitudes in Nepal because of the sheer diversity
of its communities, the disparity between rich and
poor, and the gulf in experience, education, and
opportunity between urban and rural dwellers.
The Nepalese attitude to life is essentially
religious, however, marked by a clear awareness of
authority and social structure. Hindu values and
attitudes predominate, and it is these that for the
time being maintain the status quo, despite
extremes in inequality.

KARMA, DHARMA, AND FATALISM

Hindus believe in reincarnation and *karma* (fate).
The way we lead our current lives has
consequences for our status in future lives. If our
situation is bad, it may be because of something
we have done in a past life. Success is good *karma*
(a reward); failure is bad *karma* (a punishment).
We can do our best to increase the influence of

good or limit the effects of bad *karma*, but ultimately we must accept our fate. This can lead to a shrugging of shoulders on the part of the Nepalese in the face of difficult situations. Fatalism helps maintain the status quo as people accept their lot.

Dharma is the obligation to accept one's condition in life and perform the duties associated with it conscientiously. The poor must fulfill their *dharma* without envy; the rich must fulfill theirs without self-criticism. There is thus no shame attached to begging—it's *karma*. Nor is there any obligation for the rich to take notice of the plight of the poor. Belief in *karma* and *dharma* effectively discourages people from crossing caste lines for social relations of any kind and goes a long way toward explaining why extreme disparities in wealth do not seem to bother anyone very much.

THE CASTE SYSTEM

Authority and social status in Nepal are dictated by the caste system. Officially abolished in 1963, in practice the caste system remains fundamental to people's understanding of the society in which they live, affecting politics, business, and social relations. It still influences who gets which job, who studies where, and who associates with whom.

THE CASTE SYSTEM

The *Muluki Ain* of 1854 codified the caste system in Nepal by putting social groups into five broad categories according to how closely they adhered to Hindu norms:

1. Wearers of the holy thread: *Bahuns, Chhetris*, Rajputs, and various Newar castes.
2. Non-enslavable *matawali* (alcohol drinkers): Magar, Gurung, some Newar.
3. Enslavable *matawali*: Limbu, Kirat, Tharu, Bhote (the latter includes Sherpas, Tamang, and others).
4. Impure but touchable: Newar service castes, butchers, washermen, tanners, and Europeans and Muslims.
5. Impure and untouchable: Parbatiya (blacksmiths, tanners, tailors) and Newar service castes (fishermen and scavengers).

The *matawali* of categories 2 and 3, apart from the Newars, incorporate the ethnic groups that had been outside the caste system prior to 1854. They were non-enslavable or enslavable presumably according to power play among the different groups at the time. Thus Gurungs could not be sold, whereas Tamang could.

The system has never been as rigid as the caste system in India, and some minorities in remote areas simply ignore it. Nevertheless, the caste system gives information about possible occupations and working activities, eating habits, and behavior. Only the highest caste, *Bahuns*, may be priests. Many of them are vegetarian, as eating meat would make them impure. At the other end of the scale, any job involving the killing or processing of animals is low in status (fishermen, butchers, leather workers, drum makers).

Physical contact with lower castes is considered to sully the purity of high castes. A high-caste person will not eat with a low-caste person, or accept water from him, although he may help himself. Intercaste marriage is still unusual, and there is very little mixing between castes socially.

The "Pork Eater"

It took us several days on a trek to work out why one of our four porter-guides, although keen to explain details of mountain scenery to us or build "campfires" with our children, refused to accept our invitation to join us for meals. When we asked, it had nothing to do with us: the other three guides, all *Bahun* or *Chhetri*, would not permit a Gurung "pork eater" to eat with them.

Members of higher castes may assume certain privileges, such as expecting instant service in a shop. Some caste groups can be recognized by other Nepalese people by the way they dress. Many surnames also immediately tell those in the know something about the caste background of those they are dealing with. It takes a long time for Westerners to become attuned to caste distinctions, but castes play an important role in Nepalese society.

THE IMPORTANCE OF THE FAMILY

The family is the most important social unit in Nepal. Families tend to be larger, especially in rural areas, and more extended than Western families. Older members of the family are much respected by younger generations, and expect to be looked after by their sons in old age. There is a clear family hierarchy, with greatest respect reserved for

the patriarch—in most cases the father, otherwise the eldest son/brother. Several generations may live under one roof. When a son marries, his wife will normally move into his parental home, where she is answerable to her mother-in-law as well as her husband. It is unusual for a young couple to set up on their own.

It is extremely important for the Nepalese to have children. Apart from meaning security in old age, sons in particular are of great religious significance, as they prepare their parents for the next life during special cremation rites. Childlessness is an unquestioned reason for divorce.

People derive strength from their family, and also bear responsibility toward it. The head of the family is ultimately responsible for the others, making all important decisions, and arranging marriage partners and sometimes jobs for family members. In return the patriarch expects respect and loyalty. What we in the West might see as blatant nepotism or even exploitation is regarded in Nepal as the familial responsibility of better-placed family members toward their relatives.

THE *APHNO MANCHE* CONCEPT—A FAMILY SUPPORT GROUP

The Nepalese will try to organize things through family members or through a select circle of people whom they know and can call upon. These may be friends, although the relationship is not always an equal one. It is reciprocal in the sense that it is based on mutual trust and respect. Benevolence and patronage are essentially offered in return for obedience and loyalty. Each of the two parties thinks of the other as an *aphno manche* ("own person").

To give an example, one family may lend money to another to build a house. In return, members of the debtor family can be called upon to do various jobs, such as helping slaughter a goat, or with heavy digging in the garden. Or a young man might be lent money to allow him to travel to the Middle East to work on building sites. In return, his younger brother may go to work for the lender as a servant. If he works hard and is obedient, he may be found a job later as an adult, so that the relationship between patron and beneficiary continues. Where we might see this as exploitation, the lender will probably consider his action to be philanthropy.

In public life, political affiliation plays a role in *aphno manche* loyalties.

THE *JAGIR* CULTURE

Closely related to the *aphno manche* phenomenon is the "*jagir* culture," a feudal system copied by the Shahs from the Indian Mughal regimes of the sixteenth and seventeenth centuries, and successively consolidated under the Ranas and the Panchayat. Its key features are preserved in Nepal's state machinery and political organizations today.

Historically, deserving vassals were rewarded by the ruler with a temporary land tenancy known as a *jagir*. The responsibilities of the *jagirdar* (official) were to raise an army in the event of war (that is, show loyalty, be the ruler's *aphno manche*) and to make a contribution to the treasury. Otherwise, the *jagirdar* was absolute ruler over his fiefdom, playing the roles of judge, tax collector, and governor.

The ministries and state organizations are today's *jagirs*. Personal connections are the key to recruitment. For selection into key ministries, a "premium" may be required. The highest premiums are exacted by the Ministries of Finance (taxes), Commerce (imports), and Forestry. Those ministries with access to foreign aid and grants are the most lucrative and thus most prestigious.

Promotions are made on the basis of points gained for seniority, years of service, and education. There are no points for a job well done. Productivity, innovation, and hard work are thus all suppressed by this system: a premium or the right connections are what may swing the balance.

Typical of this culture is the idea, "A government employee (*jagirdar*) is not a public servant, the public serves him." Another management saying is that "The work that gets done is the work that is rewarded." In the case of a District Forest Officer, this means cutting down trees rather than planting them; in the case of the tax official, it means harassing businessmen into "making a donation."

A government employee would lose face if he were not able to extend favors such as jobs to his political supporters or family. Temporary positions may be created even where there is no work.

Officials are not held accountable and so have little sense of responsibility.

As civil servants are rotated in their positions every two years in Nepal—ironically enough, to prevent corruption—there is no continuity. The effect is devastating, since it prevents people from developing a vision for the future, or initiating and implementing change. In a worst-case scenario, officials have two years to make good the premium they paid in the first place!

RESPECT

Respect is a key value in Nepal. It is mutual respect that has allowed the multitude of different cultural, ethnic, and religious groups to coexist peacefully for centuries. Perhaps the most important form of respect is the tradition of respect for one's elders. Age is not a cause of embarrassment in Nepal, but a requirement for respect. This is reflected in forms of address used to speak even to complete strangers. If you are perceived to be older than the person addressing you, they will call you *Didi*, meaning "older sister," or *Dai* ("older brother"). You may also be addressed as "Uncle" or "Auntie." These are entirely respectful terms. Similarly, a *-jee* suffix added to someone's name when you address them is a mark of respect. It may be attached to a first name ("John-*jee*") or to a surname ("Brown-*jee*").

Caste status, wealth, and success also command respect. Someone who is wealthy and successful is a *thulo manche* ("great/important person"). It is not necessarily important how the wealth or success has been created.

Contradictory attributes may draw respect. Wealth is respected, and yet so is self-denial and humility. This is seen in the respect shown to penniless *sadhus* (wise men and ascetics) who wander from house to house seeking alms.

MAINTAINING FACE

Tied in with notions of respect is the importance of maintaining face. The Nepalese do not like to criticize, contradict, or disagree with a person directly, because this would cause them to lose face. Nor do they like to admit not understanding something, as they themselves then lose face.

They rarely say "No" directly. An evasive answer may well be an attempt to make "No" more palatable. Be prepared for ambiguity and aware that people may tell you what they think you want to hear.

TRADITION AND SUPERSTITION

The Nepalese set great store by tradition. Many traditions are respected in an almost superstitious belief that doing things according to tradition will bode well for the future. The date for a wedding is traditionally always fixed by a priest and according to astrology. Most traditions are religious; some are to do with rites of passage. Some of the most important are described later.

ATTITUDES TOWARD WORK AND KEEPING UP APPEARANCES

Caste status and a person's level of success determine what work or activities he or she is likely to be willing to participate in. It no longer befits the status of someone who has earned a degree to perform manual work or get himself dirty. The boss commands respect, even if he is not actually seen to do very much all day. It befits his status to delegate to other people. A successful, wealthy man is unlikely to wind down on the weekend by doing a bit of gardening—he would lose standing by doing so. Nor is he likely to be a DIY enthusiast.

This attitude is why you will occasionally see people with one or more particularly long fingernails. These are a status symbol, showing that the person does not have to work with his hands. Office jobs in towns are the jobs of choice. Government employees such as

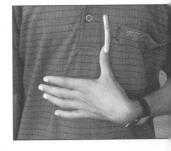

doctors or teachers sent to work in remote areas consequently often fail to turn up.

Nepalese women like to show their status by donning fine clothes and jewelry when they go out. Traditionally they own only the jewelry given to them by their husbands. The more gold they wear, the wealthier their husband.

The tall, sticklike cover girls of the Western world have little allure for the Nepalese. A few extra pounds in weight are a sign of wealth, and the adjectives *moto* (for men), meaning "well-fleshed," and *moti* (for women) are entirely positive.

ATTITUDES TOWARD WOMEN

In some Nepalese subcultures women enjoy a high status. Generally, however, women are disadvantaged both legally and socially. The law has only recently changed to allow a woman not married by the age of thirty-five to inherit an equal share from her parents. Her dowry is otherwise her share, and as this constitutes a considerable expense to her family, the birth of a boy is preferred.

Gender determination clinics exist, and female feticide is undoubtedly an issue. Women suspected of having an abortion may be imprisoned. Girl trafficking to brothels in India is also a problem.

According to a Nepalese saying, "Having a daughter is like planting a seed in another man's garden." Girls officially change families upon marriage. They enter their husband's family at the lowest level, gaining in status only when they produce a child, preferably a son. They are expected to defer to their husbands and in-laws at all times. Daughters do however maintain a special relationship with their *maiti* (maternal home), and when permitted to visit after marriage, they are likely to be treated there as princesses, higher in status than their sisters-in-law.

Menstruating women or those who have just

given birth are considered *jiuto* (impure) and must in extreme cases leave the house for a few days in order not to sully the purity of their husbands. There is however another side to this: women are not permitted to prepare food during menstruation and are allowed to rest while their husbands do the cooking.

There is still a much higher level of illiteracy among women. Increasing access to education has, however, improved the position of women. A good education ensures that a daughter will make a better marriage. Wealthy and high-caste women are not generally expected to work. In some cases a husband might lose face if his wife worked.

Divorce is very uncommon. It is difficult for a divorced woman to return to her original family and she will be expelled by her husband's. Children may remain with their mother until the age of six, after which they "belong" to their father.

Widows are shunned by society. They may well be thrown out by their husband's family as an extra mouth to feed. It is believed they are responsible for their husbands' deaths, and in extreme cases they may even be called witches.

Attitudes to women are slowly beginning to change now that more women contribute to the family income. Western women are unlikely to experience discrimination, apart from occasionally being ignored if in the company of a man.

ATTITUDES TOWARD CHILDREN

Despite their love of children, many Nepalese do not see anything wrong in children being put to work (*karma* again).

Although such industries as carpet makers are now careful not to show children working, you will not infrequently see

children working as vendors, in the kitchens of hotels, or sitting under a tailor's sewing machine on the street, helping out with hand stitching. Many are also employed as servants. What we see as child labor and exploitation is likely to be seen in Nepal as giving a poor child a chance, as he/she in many cases lives in and is fed, clothed, and possibly even sent to school by his or her employers.

ATTITUDES TOWARD NEIGHBORING COUNTRIES

Strong ethnic, religious, and trade links have existed for centuries between Nepal and Tibet. Tibetans are perceived to be industrious and skilled tradesmen. Thanks to the efforts of refugees from the Chinese annexation of Tibet in 1951, carpets are now one of Nepal's most successful exports.

Nepalese attitudes toward their Indian neighbors are ambivalent. Historically, the Nepalese are wary of their much more powerful neighbor. Several of the key demands of the Maoist insurgents relate to Nepal's "antinational and dangerous" relationship with India. Indian investors are often perceived as colonialist predators exploiting cheap Nepalese labor and exerting too much influence on politics and society. It does not help that many Indians have spilled over from the Ganges plains to settle in the Terai, competing for ever scarcer land with Nepalese who have come down from the mountains. If anything goes wrong or missing, there is a tendency to blame unknown Indian scapegoats.

On the other hand, Indian investment in Nepal is huge; India is one of the country's most important trading partners and markets, and Indians make up the biggest single group of tourists entering the country each year. There is also a large Nepalese diaspora in India, and intermarriage is not uncommon. Much of the Terai has an Indian "feel," with families, customs, and languages straddling the border.

ATTITUDES TOWARD OTHERS

The Nepalese are fiercely proud of their sovereignty and do not take kindly to interference of any sort. Foreigners are not permitted to buy land or property in Nepal and there are restrictions on the length of time foreigners may legally reside in the country. These regulations were introduced to prevent outside influence becoming too strong.

However, the fact that Nepal was never a colony means that people are not suspicious of foreigners as they might be in other developing countries. Westerners are met with a refreshing openness and self-confidence based on equality.

Theoretically, Muslims and Europeans fall into a lower-caste category, but physical contact with them does not necessarily lead to impurity. Some members of higher castes may not accept water from a Westerner, and in certain remote districts Westerners may be treated as untouchables and not permitted to enter the houses of higher-caste people. Visitors should in any case be careful not to offend religious sensibilities. Entry to certain temples is forbidden. You should always wait to be invited into people's kitchens, as the hearth is sacred. Your presence may be considered to sully the purity of the kitchen, necessitating a religious ceremony performed by a high priest to restore it.

Normally, however, you will be met with friendliness and smiles wherever you go. The Nepalese are courteous and extremely hospitable. They are not, as in some other countries, generally out for what they can get. They will treat you with respect, and with interest rather than envy. And they will expect respect in return.

Despite the ethnic mix and history of cultural tolerance, attitudes in Nepal are not without a racial element. Darker skins are still associated with inferiority. Servants or lower-caste people who labor away for hours in the sun are usually darker than people of higher status. Fair complexions are considered desirable in potential marriage partners.

Nepal gained a slightly permissive reputation during the 1970s, when Kathmandu's Jhhonchen Tole became a stop on the international hippie trail and acquired the name "Freak Street." This is, however, misleading. The hashish-smoking *sadhus* of Pashupatinath do so for religious reasons. They are respected for their asceticism, humility, and wisdom. People dress modestly, conservatively, and, especially women, generally in Nepalese style, that is, a sari or *kurta suruval* (long tunic over trousers), although the cities are not immune to Western fashions.

Displays of physical intimacy in public are taboo for anyone. Homosexuality is illegal. It is however considered perfectly normal for friends of the same sex to hold hands in public.

TIME

Time is *not* of the essence in Nepal. If you drop in on someone, they will expect to make you tea and spend time with you. Conversely, if you receive an unexpected visitor, they may not understand if you are too busy to spend time with them. This has to do with Nepalese ideals of hospitality, and the belief that the opportunity to do what is meant to be done will come around again.

It can be difficult to persuade people to commit themselves to a specific time. Partly because of the *aphno manche* system, there is little competition between craftsmen—and so little incentive for them to improve their services or get jobs done rapidly. The positive side to this is that the pace of life precludes the hectic activity of the developed world. The Nepalese word for "tomorrow" is *bholi*; "the day after tomorrow" is *parsi*. What you are most likely to hear when you ask when something will be done is *bholi-parsi*, however—which effectively means "some time after the day after tomorrow!"

chapter three

RELIGION, CUSTOMS,
& TRADITION

Until officially secularized in April 2006, Nepal
was the only Hindu kingdom in the world, its king
held to be a reincarnation of Vishnu. Hinduism
has, however, rubbed shoulders over the centuries
with the Buddhism of the Tibeto-Burmese
peoples, who make up a sizeable minority. Both
creeds have incorporated aspects of the other,
making religion in Nepal a unique and complex
blend of traditions, beliefs, practices, and rituals.

Religious tolerance and mutual respect
allow Hindus, Buddhists, Muslims, and others to
live together in peace, although conversions are
not officially recognized and proselytization
is in fact illegal. According to the census of 2001,
80.6 percent of Nepalis give their religion as
Hindu, 10.7 percent as Buddhist, 4.2 percent as
Muslim, and 4.5 percent belong to other
religions. This chapter will concentrate on
Hinduism and Buddhism, the two religions that
do most to define the nature of the country and
its people.

HINDUISM

Unlike other world religions, Hinduism cannot be traced back to a particular founder. In the absence of a strict dogma, it has assimilated various currents of thought over millennia, to a certain extent incorporating other creeds rather than suppressing them, without seeming to discard very much on the way. The result is a highly complex philosophical, religious, and social system. For Hindus the religion has a clear underlying structure, focusing as much on actions as on beliefs. Thus people with apparently contradictory beliefs may still consider themselves to be Hindu. Historically, Hinduism developed in three stages.

The Vedic Era

This period dates from approximately 1500 BCE to 900 BCE, when Aryan invaders swept into the Indian sub-continent from Central Asia to subjugate the native Dravidians. Their Vedic nature gods, such as Surya (sun) and Indra (rain), were immortalized in the four *Vedas* (Books of Wisdom), the earliest Hindu scriptures, thought to have been written between the twelfth and eighth centuries BCE. Four broad caste groups were established at this time: *Brahmins* (priests) (called *Bahuns* in Nepal), *Chhetris* (warriors and rulers), *Vaisyas* (traders and farmers), and *Sudras* (artisans and menial workers).

The Brahmanist Period

This age (900–500 BCE) was characterized by the increasing importance of ritual and priests. By ensuring that only the highest caste, the *Brahmins*, were responsible for the carrying out of religious ceremonies, the Aryans were able to maintain their hold on power. It is no coincidence that Buddhism developed at this time, finding ways to salvation without dependence on priests.

Modern Hinduism

The form of Hinduism practiced today developed around 400–200 BCE as a reaction to this ascetic movement and in a return to the original values of the *Vedas*.

Fundamental Beliefs

Hindus believe in the existence of an impersonal, all-pervading reality, Brahman. He provides a

continuous, endless cycle of genesis and demise. Brahman is manifested on Earth as the eternal order of *dharma*, which makes life and the universe possible (see page 41). The entire living world is understood as a single organism with different but related life forms, all subordinate to the principles of creation and destruction. Humankind is high up in the rankings, but not the crown of creation. Our world is the center of the cosmos. There is also an underworld full of devils and hells, while the gods are to be found in various heavens above the Earth. They too are subject to the cyclical principle.

The soul is also part of the cycle and therefore eternal. As it can move between different forms of life, there is a close relationship between humans and animals, reflected in such gods as Hanuman the monkey god, and Ganesh the elephant-headed god, but also in respect for all forms of life.

The soul of each individual being is like a lost fragment of the soul of the universe. The ultimate goal is to attain *moksha*, or release from the eternal cycle, when the individual soul is reunited with the absolute soul (Brahman). In order to achieve this, it must go through a series of rebirths, known as *sansara*, ideally moving up the social scale with each reincarnation. Where the soul next finds a home depends on how well the living being fulfills its *dharma* in its current existence.

This causal correlation, or *karma*, is one of the most important fundamentals of Hinduism and it is deeply anchored in the caste structure. Each person has a fixed position in the social hierarchy, determined by the extent to which the soul conformed to *dharma* in its previous existence. Thus a low-caste Hindu must accept his or her lot to atone for sins in a previous life. By following *dharma* dutifully a person may hope to achieve a higher status in the next life.

Hindu Obligations

Hindus have certain obligations or debts. One is to the gods, and should be met through daily acts of worship, the following of rituals, and the offering of sacrifices. Second, their debt to "the sages" is to be met by studying the *Vedas* and adhering to the rules and regulations of the caste system; and the third is an obligation to their ancestors to marry within their caste to produce a male heir who will carry on the family line and, most importantly, perform the cremation rites necessary for ascension into the next life. These obligations are not universal, but particular to each individual in his or her personal situation. A *Bahun* priest must not therefore eat meat or take life, as this would destroy the purity he needs in order to be able to worship on behalf of his community. The *Chhetri* or warrior caste, on the other hand, must protect others; thus, it is not inconceivable that they may take life.

THE HOLY COW

The veneration of the cow is an important tenet of Hinduism. The cow is regarded as a symbol of motherhood and fertility, and the killing of a cow, even by accident, is considered to be one of the most serious of religious transgressions.

The Hindu Gods of Nepal

Hinduism is both monotheistic and polytheistic. It incorporates a vast pantheon of gods and goddesses with different attributes, and yet these are merely the expression of different aspects of a single, supreme absolute, Brahman. The basic Hindu *Trimurti* ("trinity" of gods) symbolizes the three aspects of the omnipresent Brahman: Brahma is the creator of the universe; Vishnu its preserver; and Shiva its destroyer.

While most Hindus recognize the existence and significance of many gods, no one is under any obligation to worship any particular god. The most popular are Vishnu, Shiva, and the Mother Goddess, Devi. All have both positive and negative characteristics, and multiple forms. Their essentially human strengths and failings make them easy to identify with, and individuals generally have a favorite. Temples tend to be devoted to a single deity.

Brahma is rarely worshipped directly (creation being largely finished with). Vishnu sometimes appears as Narayan, the "sleeping Vishnu," recumbent on the cosmic ocean. He is also worshipped in the form of ten incarnations, including Krishna, the popular cowherd hero of the great Hindu epic the *Mahabharata*, Rama, hero of the *Ramayana*, and the Buddha: this last represents an attempt on the part of Hinduism to incorporate aspects of Buddhism.

Shiva is both creator and destroyer. He is often symbolized by a phallic lingam for his creative role, and has many different manifestations. In a good mood he appears as the peaceful Pashupati, lord of the beasts and one of the most popular gods in Nepal. Pashupatinath in Kathmandu is the most important Hindu temple in Nepal, drawing pilgrims from all over Nepal and India. Shiva is also known as Nataraja, the cosmic dancer who created the world and was believed to smoke hashish. Shiva in a filthy mood is Bhairab, often featured with multiple arms and weapons, standing over a corpse, and wearing a necklace or belt made of skulls.

A certain iconography associated with each god can help with identification. Each god has a "vehicle" (an animal) and a *shakti* (consort or female counterpart) with certain attributes and abilities. Each god is often also depicted holding certain typical objects or symbols—e.g., a conch or lotus flower for Vishnu, a trident for Shiva.

Shaktis are the creative or reproductive energies of the gods, without which they are neither complete nor effective. *Shaktis* also have different manifestations. If Shiva is the god of both creation and destruction, it is often his *shakti*, Parvati, manifesting as the goddesses Durga or Kali, who actually does the destroying. Kali demands blood sacrifices and wears a garland of skulls. The second-most important Hindu temple in Nepal, at Dakshinkali just outside Kathmandu, is dedicated to Kali. Animal sacrifices take place here regularly throughout the year.

Shaktism is a mystical form of both Buddhism and Hinduism, in which believers seek salvation in certain rituals and magic practices, including the sexual rites of the Tantra cult and worship of the *Kumari*, or Living Goddess (see pages 73–4).

How Nepalese Hindus Worship
Religion is an integral part of daily routine for most Nepalese. The day often starts with an act of worship. If you stay near a temple, you can expect to be woken early by the bells, the ringing of which brings the worshiper closer to the gods. Many Nepalese have a small shrine at home, where *puja* (offerings) of rice or fruit and colored powder are made each day to the favorite deity of the household. It is generally the wife who makes these offerings. The powder is then used to administer a *tikka* (red mark) to the forehead of each member of the family as a sign of daily communion with the gods. This takes place

after washing and before eating. Guests are also likely to receive a *tikka*.

The temple is not only a place of worship. It is also a cultural center and meeting place. Although the inner courtyards of certain temples (at Pashupatinath in Kathmandu, for example) are off-limits to non-Hindus, visitors are generally welcome and may even be invited to participate. Shoes should be removed before entering any temple building. Especially at temples dedicated to female deities, goats or chickens are sacrificed on special occasions.

The obligatory Hindu veneration of priests includes the offering of hospitality to priests and *sadhus* or *gurus* (teachers and spiritual guides). These are individual, male ascetics who have embarked upon a spiritual search and live from alms. They go from door to door, dressed in little more than a loincloth, and with few possessions apart from the small cooking pot in which they collect small handfuls of rice. They are respected figures, not beggars, and perform spiritual ceremonies if required.

Some of the most fundamental ceremonies for every Hindu are those associated with rites of passage. These start at birth with a blessing and naming ceremony, and continue the first time a baby is fed solid food (rice). Relatives and friends bring money and gifts and the baby is expected to receive a spoonful of rice from each guest. Later there are ceremonies to mark the first time a boy has his hair cut, and purification after a girl first menstruates. Other significant ceremonies are marriage, blessings upon a pregnancy, and finally, cremation, including the sprinkling of ashes in a holy river, and annual offerings to deceased ancestors. If possible, these last should be made by the eldest son, so that the soul of his father can pass from a state of limbo to rebirth. Newar girls also celebrate *Ihi*, their symbolic marriage to the god Vishnu between the ages of seven and eleven, which is to protect them from the stigma of widowhood. As they are married to an immortal god, they cannot become widows.

BUDDHISM

As a form of teaching that aims to show the way to salvation, Buddhism in fact follows the same goal as Hinduism. It also adheres to the basic principles of *karma* and reincarnation. Buddhism dispenses with the mediating role of priests and the caste system, however.

The religion's founder, Siddhārtha Gautama Buddha (*c.* 563–483 BCE), gave up worldly goods and pleasures to become an ascetic in his search for enlightenment. When this failed to work, he developed his "Middle Way" of meditation. He recognized "Four Noble Truths," teaching that life means suffering because of our sensual desires and the illusion that they are important. We can only

escape this suffering by renouncing the pleasures of the world and by following the "Eightfold Path" of right understanding, right aspiration, right speech, right action, right livelihood, right effort, right thought, and right contemplation to selflessness and liberation from suffering. Salvation of the soul is achieved when the soul enters *nirvana* (literally "drifting/fading away"), a state in which all earthly desires are extinguished and the cycle of reincarnation is broken. To achieve *nirvana* it is necessary to go through a series of rebirths, but this is not simply fate, because what people do in one life will influence what role they play in the next. In contrast to Hinduism, the individual soul is not eternal and unchangeable, but formed according to the laws of *karma* when a person dies.

The Buddha himself never wrote down his teachings, and two main forms of Buddhism developed after his death. The first, the Hinayana, held that it was the role of the individual to attain *nirvana*. Later, in the first century BCE, the Mahayana, or "large vehicle" school of Buddhism, emerged, pleading for the collective attainment of *nirvana*. The most important change they made was in introducing the *Bodhisattva*: someone who has achieved enlightenment but who elects not to enter *nirvana*, but to show others the way to salvation. The most revered of these is Avalokiteshvara, representing compassion. Over time, Mahayana Buddhism incorporated not only the *Bodhisattvas*, but also various Hindu gods. Their physical representations in temples and shrines in combination with rituals and a rich mythology made them more accessible to people than the abstract philosophy of "the enlightened one."

Vajrayana (thunderbolt, or diamond vehicle) or tantric Buddhism began to be practiced in Nepal from around the eighth century CE. This is an esoteric school in which mystical forces, rituals, and sexual practices play an important role. Tantric rituals have also had great influence on some forms of Hinduism. Tantrism is based on the interwovenness of all things. Devotees are led to salvation through reading scriptures, reciting holy *mantras* (sacred words used as an object of concentration), contemplating *mandalas* (holy pictures of gods or their symbols), and carrying out ritual movements (*mudra*).

OM MANI PADME HUM

All visitors to Nepal are likely to become familiar with the most famous, most used *mantra*, the Bodhisattva Avalokiteshvara's "*Om Mani Padme Hum*," to be heard at any of the main Buddhist sites in Kathmandu, but also emanating from any shop selling Nepali music to tourists. Literally it means "Oh you jewel in the lotus flower." For Buddhists, however, it is symbolic of universal godly power, all-embracing love, and the universe in its physical and psychic infinity.

Prevalent in parts of northern Nepal and the Kathmandu valley is Tibetan Buddhism, under the spiritual leadership of the Dalai Lama. It draws on aspects of the ancient "Bon" religion of Tibet, the religious practices of the Himalayan peoples (shamanism, animism, nature religions, etc.), and the "vehicles" of Mahayana and Vajrayana Buddhism.

How Buddhists Worship

In a spiritual practice called circumambulation, it is usual to walk clockwise around all Buddhist temples, because this follows the sun's course: Buddha is the sun of enlightenment in people's hearts. Prayer wheels are a feature of all Buddhist temples. These often elaborately carved metal cylinders contain rolls

of paper wrapped round an axis, on which holy
mantras are written many times. The wheels are
often mounted in rows near the entrance to stupas,
to be turned by people during circumambulation as
a means of spreading spiritual blessings and well-

being. The prayer
wheels, flags, *thangkas*
(religious paintings),
and murals in
monasteries are all seen
as aids to meditation,
bringing the devout
closer to the godly.

SYNCRETISM

If religious tolerance is a feature in Nepal, so too
is syncretism. Hinduism and Buddhism have
intermingled in Nepal to such a degree over the
centuries that if you ask a Nepali if he is Hindu or
Buddhist, you may well get the answer "Yes!"

Hindus and Buddhists in Nepal share temples,
gods, symbols, and festivals. Hindu gods may be
depicted in Buddhist temples, and Buddhist stupas
may be found in Hindu temples. In Pashupatinath,
the Shiva lingam is covered once a year with a mask
of the Buddha. At the important Buddhist stupa of
Swayambhunath, Hindus worship the god of
Swayambhunath as "Sambu" (Shiva). For
Buddhists, Swayambhu is the Buddha. Buddhists

see an aspect of the Bodhisattva Avalokiteshvara in Lokeshvara, "the lord of the world," whereas Hindus see him as a manifestation of Shiva in the form of a Buddhist god.

The goddesses Kali and Durga also often merge with the Buddhist goddess Tara, the most

important female Bodhisattva. Female goddesses are often perceived to be variants of the Divine Mother, particularly in tantrism. The erotic carvings on the roof beams of many temples are also common to both religions and stem from Hindu tantrism, which was adapted by Buddhism.

Nowhere is the syncretism between the two religions clearer than among the Newar people of the Kathmandu valley. Newars may be Hindus or Buddhists. In practice the issue of "which religion" does not seem relevant to many Newars. They worship a plethora of hybrid gods that may or may not be recognized by purists of one religion or the other! Marriage between Hindus and Buddhists of the same caste is not a problem. Newar Hindus may feel closer to Newar Buddhists than to other Nepalese Hindus, simply because they speak the same language and share their cultural heritage.

> **THE CULT OF THE LIVING GODDESS**
> A further example of the hybrid nature of the
> Newar religion is the cult of the Living
> Goddess, or *Kumari*—one of the most
> fascinating aspects of religion in Nepal. The
> most important *Kumari* is the *Kumari* Devi,
> or "Royal *Kumari*," who lives in a house
> known as the *Kumari* Ghar on the edge of
> Kathmandu's Durbar Square.

The *Kumari* is believed to be the bodily
incarnation of the goddess Taleju, a manifestation
of Durga. Although Taleju is a Hindu goddess,
the *Kumari* is always selected from the Newar
Buddhist *Sakhya* caste of goldsmiths and
silversmiths. For Buddhists she is the tantric
goddess Vajradevi.

The *Kumari* is selected in early childhood
from a group of candidates who take part in a
secret ritual conducted by priests, which includes
being left in a room full of severed water buffalo
heads, the theory being that if she is really a
reincarnation of the bloodthirsty goddess Durga,
she will not mind!

She lives in seclusion, away from her family, in
the service of religion. She leaves her house very
rarely, traditionally to perform religious duties
such as legitimizing the rule of the king by
administering a *tikka* to his forehead as a symbol

of the Third Eye of
Wisdom, on the
occasion of the Indra
Jatra festival. She is
believed to have great
power and is widely
worshipped by
both Hindus and
Buddhists, who will
wait under her
windows hoping for

a glimpse of her. As soon as she begins
menstruating or loses blood by injury, she returns
to her family and is replaced.

ISLAM AND OTHER RELIGIONS

The first Muslims to arrive in Nepal were traders
from Kashmir and India, who came between the
fifteenth and seventeenth centuries. The
descendants of these early Muslim settlers speak
Nepali and are not easy to distinguish from high-
caste Hindus. After the Indian Mutiny of 1857,
many more came north to escape the violence and
settled in the Terai. They maintain close links to
communities across the border in Bihar and Uttar
Pradesh. Unlike in India, in Nepal they have
coexisted in peace with their Hindu neighbors.

There are a small number of practicing
Christians in Nepal, who tend to meet in private

houses. In rural areas, aspects of shamanistic or animalist religions continue to be practiced.

RELIGIOUS TRADITIONS AND RITES OF PASSAGE

Religion is such an important aspect of life in Nepal that it is sometimes said that "every other building is a temple, and every other day is a festival." There are hundreds of religious festivals throughout the year. Most are related to Hindu or Buddhist gods or tradition, but some honor personal relatives or ancestors, while others mark the passing of the seasons or agricultural cycles. They may be celebrated at temples or other religious sites (such as rivers), or at home. Some are celebrated countrywide, others are regional. Many involve ritual bathing and most culminate in feasting within the family. They are part of the common heritage, and bring people together whatever their creed or ethnic or cultural background.

Be sure to join in! Nepalese hospitality, inclusiveness, and a genuine eagerness to share their culture mean that you are likely to be invited to participate in proceedings. This can be an enlightening experience, and it is always enjoyable.

Businesspeople or those operating to a tight schedule should be aware that the country may come to a complete standstill for days at a time during festivals. This can be a problem especially during Dasain and Tihar, celebrated in September and late October/early November, when it is traditional for people to return to their ancestral home or visit family. Some of the most important festivals are given below.

THE NEPALESE CALENDAR

Officially Nepal follows the Vikram Sambat solar calendar, which is fifty-seven years ahead of the Gregorian calendar. The Nepalese year begins in mid-April and consists of twelve months that are out of step with the Western ones. Thus the Nepali year 2064 began in April 2007. Most religious festivals, however, are calculated by astrologers according to a lunar calendar, so dates can vary. Things are further complicated by the fact that Newars follow their own calendar, celebrating their new year in November, and the Tibetan peoples of the mountains follow a different calendar again.

January/February

Basant Panchami marks the beginning of spring and is devoted to Saraswati, the goddess of learning. Schoolchildren make offerings at her shrines to bring success in learning.

Losar, the Tibetan New Year, is observed by Tibeto-Burmese people with folk songs and dancing at the new moon in February. Hundreds of lamas and traditionally-dressed Tibetans circumambulate the stupa at Bodhnath in Kathmandu.

February/March

Shivaratri brings thousands of *sadhus* and other pilgrims from all over Nepal and India to Pashupatinath. People bathe in the Bagmati. At night, hundreds of oil lamps are lit and an all-night vigil is held.

Also known as the Festival of Colors, **Holi** heralds the beginning of spring and looks forward to the coming harvest. People roam the streets throwing colored powder and water at each other. Foreigners are likely to be special targets. It is all very good-natured, but be prepared to throw your clothes away afterward, or don't go out.

At the festival of **Rato Machhendranath**, the image of this god is transported around Patan on a tall, precarious-looking wooden chariot that dwarfs the men heaving it along on its solid wooden wheels. This god is believed to have great influence over the monsoon. For Buddhists Machhendranath is Lokeshvara, lord of the world. The festival is thus celebrated by both Hindus and Buddhists, and was traditionally attended by the king, and the *Kumari Devi*, who gave the king her blessing.

April/May

Bisket Jatra marks the Nepali New Year, which starts at the beginning of the Nepali month Baisakh, more or less in the middle of April. This is an official public holiday. In Bhaktapur the fierce, angry god Bhairab is taken for a ride around the town on another cumbersome chariot. A huge lingam is erected on the riverbank, only to be pulled down again the next day in a tug-of-war.

Mani Rimdu is a three-day Sherpa festival at the full moon in May and celebrates the vanquishing of the ancient Tibetan Bon religion by Buddhism.

Buddha Jayanti is celebrated by both Hindus and Buddhists to mark the birth, enlightenment, and death of Buddha (a reincarnation of Vishnu for Hindus).

July/August

At the festival of **Janai Purnima**, *Bahun* and *Chhetri* men change the *janai* (sacred thread) that they wear from left shoulder to right hip to symbolize purity. Everyone is given a thread to be tied around their wrist on this day as a protective talisman for the rest of the year.

Gai Jatra venerates the cow. The Newar people believe that cows will lead them to the next world after death. Those who have lost relatives during the previous year join a procession of people leading cows through the streets of Kathmandu in order to facilitate their deceased relatives' passage into the next world. Later, people wear cow masks, and the tradition is to exchange silly jokes!

August/September

Teej is a special, three-day festival for women, involving feasting, fasting, ritual bathing to wash away sin, and dancing. They pray for the longevity of their husbands and the success of their marriages. After bathing, they traditionally don all the red and gold finery of their wedding day. Western women are welcome spectators and may well be invited to join in.

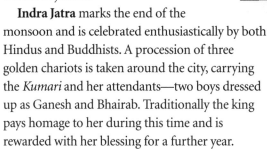

Indra Jatra marks the end of the monsoon and is celebrated enthusiastically by both Hindus and Buddhists. A procession of three golden chariots is taken around the city, carrying the *Kumari* and her attendants—two boys dressed up as Ganesh and Bhairab. Traditionally the king pays homage to her during this time and is rewarded with her blessing for a further year.

September–December

Dasain is the most important festival in Nepal. The country virtually shuts down and traffic conditions are chaotic beforehand as everyone makes the effort to get home. People celebrate by eating good food and buying new clothes. It takes place after the monsoon, in late September or early October. It is also known as Durga Puja, as it celebrates the slaying of the buffalo demon Mahisasura by this goddess.

Certain days of Dasain are more significant than others. On the first day the devout bathe and plant barley in sand and water taken from the river. On the seventh day, *Fulpati* ("sacred flowers"), flowers are brought from the old palace of Prithvi Narayan Shah at Gorkha to the king at Hanuman Dhoka in Kathmandu. The eighth day is *Kala Ratri* ("black night"), when eight buffaloes and a hundred-and-eight goats are decapitated in Durbar Square, Kathmandu, ideally with one chop of the knife.

This is one festival in which it is impossible to

avoid guts and gore, so if you are at all squeamish, don't go out! Temples are awash in sacrificial blood on the ninth day, when literally thousands of goats meet their end—thirty-five to forty thousand goats are slaughtered on that day in the town of Pokhara alone. The tools of a person's trade (guns for a soldier, a saw for a carpenter) are then sprinkled with sacrificial blood in the hope that Durga will bless their usefulness and accuracy. Blood is also sprinkled on all vehicles (including the aircraft of Nepal

Airlines) to safeguard against accidents, and if you take a closer look at the clear, plastic-covered "padlock chains" draped around parked motorcycles and bicycles, you'll find they are actually the cleaned out intestines of a goat!

Not many Nepalis eat a lot of meat but at Dasain, most people will have goat for dinner. Family visits are made on the tenth day and parents put *tikkas* on their children's foreheads and shoots of the barley planted on the first day in their hair.

Tihar, also known as the Festival of Lights, lasts five days and is celebrated toward the end of October or early November. On the first day, crows (messengers of the god of death) are honored. On the second day, dogs, though kicked out of the way throughout the rest of the year, are honored for their role in guiding the deceased across the river of the dead. Cows are garlanded on the third day, bullocks on the fourth, and the fifth day is called *Bhai Tikka* (Brothers' Day), when sisters honor their brothers with *tikkas* and blessings, and gifts are exchanged. On the third, most important day, also known as *Lakshmi Puja*, people light up their homes with candles and wick lamps in order to usher in Lakshmi, the goddess of wealth. As with many festivals, Tihar ends with a family feast.

Sita Bibaha Panchami recalls the marriage of Rama and Sita and is celebrated mainly in Janakpur, birthplace of Sita, in late November or early December.

chapter four

MAKING FRIENDS

MEETING NEPALIS

Although socializing in Nepal tends to focus on the extended family, the Nepalese also like to spend time with friends. Friends expect to look after each other, enjoy life together, share significant moments such as success at school or an engagement, and support each other in times of need. Women friends are important in supporting a bride when she leaves home for good. Later, family may take precedence over friendships, particularly for women, who generally move away from their childhood friends upon marriage. Background (caste) remains a key factor in any friendship, and political affiliation may also play a role. Close friendship between people of disparate backgrounds is unusual, as are friendships between unrelated men and women, although things are changing, particularly in urban areas.

Socializing takes place mainly at home, although people may meet at cafés or restaurants in urban areas. Increasingly popular venues, especially for the young, are Western-style cafés such as ice-cream parlors or pizzerias. These are places to be seen, whereas more traditional Nepalese restaurants often offer more discreet facilities, with some tables screened off or in small wooden pavilions. People may also congregate at the temple, water pump, or another central place to talk or watch the world go by. On specific occasions or festivals such as Tihar they may meet at the market to admire decorated shop fronts, as well as to "see and be seen."

The vast majority of Nepalese people are open and friendly, although you may find yourself worthy of a few stares in areas off the tourist track. Urban, educated Nepalese will engage you in conversation (in English), and you are likely to be accosted by the friendly shouts of children wherever you go. Although a small minority of these might be looking for sweets, pens, or a few hours' employment as a guide, most simply want to practice their English and are genuinely interested in you and where you come from. They are usually also quite happy to answer your questions. Communication with those who have not been to school is obviously more difficult unless you speak Nepalese, but any effort to do so is much appreciated, and if you stay anywhere for a while, you will soon find everyone knows you.

If a Nepalese person in your home country gives you the contact details of a family member, you can expect to be received by them as a friend. They will do whatever they can to help you, and will probably introduce you to other family members.

It takes time, however, to establish truly close friendships. This is due partly to language barriers, but to a certain extent also to cultural differences. Conversations may remain at a superficial level for a long time. It is probably easiest to get to know people in a working situation, where you automatically have a common purpose and basis for cooperation. Other ways of making friends may be to take some language lessons, possibly from someone equally eager to learn your language, or to suggest cooking together: people are interested in what Westerners eat, and are both delighted and amused to be asked to explain what to do with the various exotic vegetables, fruits, and spices available at the market.

GREETINGS AND OTHER COURTESIES

To greet and to say good-bye in Nepal you put the palms of your hands together in front of your chest, as if praying, and say *Namaste.* This literally means "I salute the godly in you." Raising the height of your hands shows increasing respect. You may also say *Namascar* to show particular respect for someone. "Ladies first" is not a maxim in Nepal.

It is polite to greet the oldest members of a group and men first, while superiors are generally greeted first by their subordinates.

WHAT SHOULD I TALK ABOUT?

If you speak a little Nepalese, small talk will do wonders for your language skills. Initial questions, posed by colleagues, neighbors, taxi drivers and shopkeepers, are likely to focus on where you come from, how long you have been in Nepal, what you are there for, your family, your job, and your diet.

A small collection of photographs of your family and home is a useful icebreaker that will stimulate conversation. Once people get to know you a little better, few topics of conversation are off-limits. An element of comparison or finding out about the other culture is inevitable and mutual. Some questions are potentially embarrassing, such as questions about your income, the price of airfares to Nepal, or other comparative costs. Given the income gap, it may be as well to understate certain costs or put things in a cultural perspective.

Sex and homosexuality are not subjects that are casually or openly discussed. Nepalis may, however, surprise you with questions on topics of a personal nature such as contraception or infertility (the latter being a reason for immediate divorce in Nepal) as they look for solutions to their problems in Western ideas. Often there is a specific reason for asking.

You should be extremely cautious about broaching subjects such as poverty, dowries, caste, corruption, the Maoist conflict, and politics in general. If talking about the Nepalese monarchy, you should be aware that, although the deposed king and his son were not as popular as their predecessors, the king is traditionally viewed as a reincarnation of Vishnu and thus has religious significance for Hindus.

HUMOR

Nepalese people are easygoing with a ready sense of humor that tends to be quite slapstick. Foreigners may find it lacking in subtlety. Few Nepalese will appreciate irony or black comedy. They take themselves quite seriously and will criticize themselves, but do not take kindly to being poked fun at (self-ridicule is safer). Western caricatures depicting politicians or royalty may be seen as irreverent. They will not tolerate even lighthearted disrespect for older members of the family or party.

NEPALESE HOSPITALITY

The Nepalese are extremely hospitable, and will probably press food and drink on you. Sometimes complete strangers will persist in inviting you to their homes. In this case it is probably as well to smile and give a vague answer: "Yes, sometime I'd love to visit you."

The etiquette of eating and drinking can be something of a minefield. If you really do not want to eat anything, smile and explain that you have just eaten. If invited to dinner at someone's house, you will be guest of honor and as such will be served first, and given the best. This can make you feel uncomfortable, as the whole family will watch you eat. Don't wait for your host to begin— only once he is sure you are enjoying your meal will the man of the house join in, followed by other male members of the family and the children. Your hostess is likely to eat the leftovers once everyone else has finished.

There is quite an art to eating with the thumb and two fingers of your right hand (the left is used for "other business" and is thus unclean), particularly when sitting cross-legged on the floor with your plate in front of you. Although no one will be offended if you ask for a spoon (knives and forks are less likely to be available), the Nepalese appreciate your making an effort to eat as they do. Eating with your mouth open and smacking noisily with your lips is quite acceptable—indeed, even a sign that you are enjoying your meal.

Avoid taking huge amounts on to your plate, as anything that has been on your plate is *jiuto* (unclean) and will be thrown away if you do not eat it. You should also be careful not to touch anyone else's glass or plate and certainly not their food, as this would also be *jiuto*. Nor should you under any circumstances step over anyone else or anyone else's plate, as this would show great disrespect.

You may be offered *raksi* to drink. This is alcohol of unpredictable strength, often home-brewed, and to be treated with caution. Often it will be passed around a party in a teapotlike metal vessel with a long narrow spout. The idea is to pour the liquid into your mouth without touching the spout: any bottle you touch with your lips is *jiuto* for other people. Jugs of water may also be passed around in this way.

If you finish everything on your plate, you will be given more. The polite way of saying you have had enough is in fact to leave a little on your plate. Your hosts will appreciate you saying "*Dherai mitho bhayo*" ("That was delicious") and "*Ucous mucous bhayo*" ("That was a lot; I'm really full").

People will welcome return invitations and generally be very interested in what you might offer them to eat. You should however check beforehand whether they eat meat, as many are vegetarian. Beef and in most cases pork should certainly be avoided.

WHAT SHOULD I WEAR?

It is always best to err on the side of modesty and formality when choosing what to wear in Nepal. The Nepalese dress up to go out. Nakedness is frowned upon, and although Nepalese women may display bare tummies between their blouse and sari, their legs and shoulders are always covered. Women should certainly wear long trousers or skirts. Coolest are often the Nepali-style *kurta suruval*—long, fine cotton trousers with a long tunic over the top—and no one will think it strange to see a Westerner in this attire. Indeed, the Nepalese are a very inclusive people, and many are delighted to see their guests in Nepalese clothing, especially at festivals. Women will probably be quite honored to be asked for their help in getting you into a sari.

Ties are not necessary except for very formal occasions—indeed, they are impractical in the heat—but a collar is advisable. The traditional *topi* (cloth hat) worn by men is a sign of respectability and should only be worn if you have been given or invited to wear one.

Shoes are considered dirty and should always be removed when entering someone's house.

GIFTS

A gift will not be expected if you are invited to visit a Nepalese family, but flowers, fruit, chocolate, or homemade cakes if you have access to an oven are always appreciated, as is a present of anything from your home country. If you stay with anyone for a while and take photographs while you are there, a small collection of these, particularly those showing both you and your hosts, is likely to go over very well. Books can also make appropriate presents. A good present for a business contact is a bottle of whiskey, although you should check first whether they drink alcohol. You should avoid gifts made of leather, especially cowhide, and anything black or white, as these are considered unlucky colors. White is the color of mourning.

NEIGHBORS

Most expatriates and wealthier Nepalis live in houses surrounded by walled gardens or yards, and you are unlikely to have much to do with your neighbors except to exchange greetings, unless you actively seek their company. However, do not be surprised if a few are bold enough to walk in unexpectedly—doorbells and the concept of knocking before entering are almost unknown.

Noise can be a cause of conflict between neighbors. It is as well to remember that the Nepalese rise at dawn. Half-past four in the morning is not too early for them to start going about their daily business.

Occasionally, private individuals may mark a forthcoming marriage or the anniversary of the death of a loved one by holding a *sabhda* (special festival). A priest is invited to their house to lead purification ceremonies that include loud prayers, chanting, and music broadcast to the entire neighborhood by means of a loudspeaker. There is little you can do about this. Complaints are unlikely to be understood and you will probably be invited to join in. *Sabhdas* can last up to a week.

EXPATRIATE ASSOCIATIONS

Expatriate communities in Nepal are small and largely concentrated in Kathmandu. Individual embassies can provide information about cultural associations. The British Council, Alliance Française, and Goethe Institute all offer library facilities and cultural programs in Kathmandu.

SPORTS AND OTHER CLUBS

The facilities you might visit in Western countries in order to meet people, such as sports or other clubs, are rare outside Kathmandu and Pokhara. Even where they exist, most of the people you will meet there are likely to be other expatriates. Nepalese women are even less likely than men to engage in sports. Having said that, groups of men and boys playing cricket or football in open spaces will probably be quite happy to let you join in, while providing a football is one fast way to acquire a young fan club!

chapter five

THE NEPALESE AT HOME

Nepalese life centers around home and the family. Several generations of a family may live in the same house, with children sleeping in their parents' rooms for years. There may be little space and no privacy. There is great interdependence, and a strict hierarchy and sense of respect for authority dictate that even adult children may still ask their parents for permission to do things. Much of life spills out on to the street.

NEPALESE HOUSING

Generally built in traditional styles with regionally available materials, Nepalese houses are as varied as the country's climate and terrain.

The standard of housing reflects extreme differences in wealth: a few very wealthy people inhabit luxurious mansions in walled compounds, while the poorest—former bonded laborers—are forced to reconstruct their shelters on the dried-up riverbed each year after the monsoon, using driftwood, plastic bags, and other debris. What you will not find in Nepal are the vast shantytowns common on the edges of some African or South American cities.

Houses reflect the fact that much of Nepalese life is conducted outside. Most are simple, rectangular constructions featuring two or three small rooms, often one behind the other and connected by a corridor which may be on the outside of the house. Staircases are also often external. An end room facing on to the street sometimes houses a small shop. Many houses look half-built: metal stays are left sticking out of their flat roofs to allow for upward expansion at a later date.

Except in wealthy homes, kitchens are primitive and may contain only a few pots and pans on open shelves, and a fireplace or kerosene stove. If there is a sink it may well be at ground level, as the Nepalese generally wash up or prepare vegetables in a squatting position. Even cold running water in the kitchen is not typical.

Wealthier people might have a (bottled) gas stove and a few electrical goods—an electric rice cooker is a coveted wedding present among the urban wealthy. Dry foods are stored in open sacks to prevent molding in the humid climate.

Vegetables and fresh foods are bought or harvested each day as far as possible. People are much more likely to have a television than a fridge, and washing machines are almost unheard of. Instead, washing is done by hand in cold water.

Generally speaking, electricity is only available in urban areas and the Terai. Power outages and surges are frequent. Water shortages also occur. Only wealthier middle-class families have running water in the house.

An indoor lavatory is a luxury. Most often it is in an outhouse at the back and may well be shared by several families. Western toilets are not common; the usual is a hole in the ground. Toilet paper is also not common, although it can be bought. Instead, water and the left hand are used (which is why it is taboo to offer anyone anything with your left hand).

In urban areas Western-style bathrooms are on the increase but, generally, the idea of sitting in your own dirty bathwater is disgusting to most Nepalese—running water is important. Many houses have no bathroom at all. Instead, people wash and do their washing at an outside tap if they have one, and otherwise at the local public water pump, even in the middle of the city. By some tacit agreement, men and women use public fountains at different times. Men strip down to a pair of shorts, while women bathe through the fabric of a long petticoat, tied around their chest, but leaving their arms free.

The Outdoor Bathroom

Where we lived on the banks of the Rapti River, the men's "bathroom" was upstream from the bridge, the women's downstream. Handfuls of twigs gathered on the way there served as toothbrushes. This was more than a mere bathroom: it was the site of ritual cleansing. Nearby were the cremation *ghats* (platforms). Further downriver still was the local car wash, where it was not unusual to see a truck or bus parked midstream.

Otherwise houses may be spartan by Western standards. Floors are often bare concrete, and furniture is minimal. Beds are simple wooden platforms that may double as sofas. They are more likely to be covered with a straw mat or simple blanket than a mattress. The Nepalese typically sit cross-legged on the floor to eat (the rich on sofas), so tables and chairs are relatively unusual.

Most Nepalese houses have a house shrine. One room may be set aside to accommodate it, or there may be a small altar set up in the kitchen. The hearth or fire in the kitchen is sacred, so you should never throw rubbish on to the hearth. Always wait to be invited to enter the kitchen or approach the house shrine.

Roof terraces accommodate water tanks and sometimes solar panels, and are used for drying clothes, as well as tomatoes, chilies, and other produce.

Organized refuse collection is not established in Nepal. Instead people burn their rubbish regularly on the street. Litter is a problem.

HOUSEHOLD DUTIES

Women carry out the bulk of household tasks, including the collection of water, firewood, and fodder for animals where required. In wealthy middle-class families, children will not be expected to make much contribution to household duties. In an extended family, the youngest daughter-in-law is the family member lowest in rank. She is likely to be expected to get up first, make everyone else's breakfast, and generally do more than her share of chores.

An estimated 20 percent of urban families employ a servant to assist with duties in the house and garden. This may be a *Didi*, but many are also children. There are estimated to be more than 56,000 children working as domestic servants in

Nepal. How they are treated depends very much on individual circumstances. Only around 30 percent of them are enrolled in school.

THE NEPALESE DAY

In general, the Nepalese are up before dawn. The cacophony begins immediately: you are likely to be woken each morning by bells being rung by early worshipers at the local temple, dogs barking, tradesmen calling, the clatter of pots and pans and thundering of buckets being filled as your immediate neighbors wash up last night's dishes, and some serious clearing of throats. (Nepalis consider our habit of blowing our noses into a handkerchief disgusting, and would expect us to throw it away. Instead, they spend several minutes hawking to clear their throat every morning, spitting out whatever comes up, as if trying to remove the dirt under their toenails from within!)

But despite the early commotion, the day begins at a more leisurely pace than life in the

West. It may start with a walk to the local temple. An early breakfast consists of a cup of *Nepali chiya*, a thick, sweet tea made with boiled milk, possibly accompanied by some puffed rice or *roti*, a flat rice pancake. Thereafter, people have time to go to the market, get on with household chores, or do homework. Schools and offices do not generally open before 10:00 a.m., giving families the time to enjoy the first of their two main meals of the day together. In high mountain areas where people are poorer and rice is scarce, this is likely to be a millet gruel. Elsewhere, *dhal baat* is the national dish and a twice-daily ritual.

People wash before and after sitting down to this large meal of *dhal* (lentils) and *baat* (rice), often accompanied by spicy vegetables and pickles. Wealthy families may have meat or fish as an accompaniment, particularly on special occasions, when a goat or water buffalo may be slaughtered. People sit cross-legged on the floor with their plate in front of them, pour the lentils over their rice, and eat by compressing small quantities of the rice and lentil mixture into mouthful-sized balls with the thumb and two fingers of the right hand. Meat or fish is eaten off the bone.

After *dhal baat*, men will leave for the office, and children for school. Mid-afternoon people eat a snack, *kaajaa*, consisting of puffed rice, a little *dahi* (yogurt) if available, or *roti*, washed down with another cup of *chiya*. Children take a similar snack to school with them.

School generally finishes at 4:00 p.m. After homework and chores, children play among themselves or watch television. Late afternoon, once the heat of the day has begun to subside, is a busy time at the market. Boys and young adults may meet for a game of football or cricket. At around seven in the evening, the family will convene again for *dhal baat*—their second and last main meal of the day.

Evenings are not long in Nepal, given the time people expect to get up, and the frequent curfews of recent years. Outside the tourist areas, all is quiet and most lights are out by ten o'clock.

EVERYDAY SHOPPING

Fruit and vegetables can be bought from peddlers pushing wheelbarrows or heavily-laden bicycles around the neighborhood, and basics are also available from small corner shops. Most shopping is done at the *bazaar*, however.

The word "*bazaar*" refers both to the town center and to the "market" as we know it. Few shopping centers or supermarkets exist outside Kathmandu, so shopping is another aspect of Nepalese life that is largely conducted out of doors. Shops are usually small and specialist: you must go to one shop for fruit, another for pulses and flour, another for toiletries, and so on. There are often several shops of a particular type in close proximity, for example, several goldsmiths' or butchers' or tailors'. This is because of the caste and family background of these

professions; the proprietors are often related.

Fresh foodstuffs are often simply laid out on the sidewalk. This includes animal carcasses, which are painted with some kind of orange preservative to keep the flies off. You can ask to have a slice chopped off. Goats and chickens may be a better bet—they can be purchased alive, or butchered as you watch. Meat and fish markets are certainly worth a look—just don't be surprised if you feel the need to turn vegetarian for a while.

Some shops sell a wide variety of imported goods such as pasta, canned foods, breakfast cereals, chocolate, sweets, and alcohol. These goods are often way beyond the means of most Nepalese, but may make a good present. Some commodities considered basics by most Westerners, including pasta, butter, cheese, and real coffee, are often not available outside

Kathmandu. The only bread available outside tourist areas is the white, sliced variety with a slightly sweet taste.

As in other areas of life in Nepal, people build up a mutually beneficial relationship with certain shopkeepers whom they consider to be their *aphno manche*. In return for regular patronage and recommendations, they may expect good quality or a good price. It is usual to ask to be shown things, rather than to take things from shelves yourself, and except where prices are marked, to haggle a little over prices.

CHILDREN

At birth babies are often whisked away from their mother to be examined, washed, and wrapped by their paternal grandmother. She generally plays a key role in bringing up the children within the extended family. Children generally sleep with their parents for several years. Few Nepalese would dream of putting a baby in a crib in a separate room. Small babies are regularly massaged with mustard oil, thought to be good for their skin, and left to bask in the warmth of the sun.

Later they may accompany various members of the extended family as they perform daily chores. They do not wear diapers—people just mop up after them where necessary. Older siblings are mobilized at an early age to look out for younger ones. Children are treated as adults from a surprisingly young age, and a sense of respect for all elders, including older siblings, is instilled into them from their earliest years.

Creative Play

Toys are rare, and children are often left to play with what they can find. This results in a great deal of inventiveness. A chain of elastic bands makes an excellent skipping rope. Tie them all together in a bundle, however, and you have a small rubber ball for practicing football skills as required!

While the children of middle-class families are not generally expected to assist with household duties, other children may well be required not only to assist with housework, but to contribute to the family income from a young age: according to UNICEF's report of 2004, *The State of the World's Children*, 31 percent of children in Nepal are involved in economic activity. The vast majority of these are engaged in agriculture, most as unpaid family workers, but large numbers also work in domestic service, factories, as child porters, in shops, hotels, the construction industry, as conductors or ticket collectors on buses, or as street vendors, ragpickers, or beggars. Many children find themselves in debt bondage—working to repay debts incurred by their families.

FAMILY EVENTS

At all social levels, the extended family will come together to celebrate certain family events or religious festivals. People don their best clothes—women their finest saris and jewelry—and *tikkas* are usually exchanged. Food is always involved and may be presented as offerings to the gods. A goat or water buffalo may be slaughtered. Often the family will also dance or sing.

MARRIAGE

As children grow up, potential marriage partners are discussed. Although love marriages are on the increase, and children may veto a marriage partner, most marriages are still arranged for children by their parents. Marriage partners are unlikely to be from the same town or known personally to the family beforehand, but are selected on the basis of recommendations from intermediaries, who may be friends or relatives.

Weddings are elaborate affairs taking place over several days. After a large party hosted by her family, and to which several hundred guests may be invited, a bride is physically picked up by a male blood relative and ceremoniously handed over to her husband and his male relatives to be taken to her new home and family.

Traditions and ceremonies differ according to the social and ethnic background of the couple, however. In Hindu communities a dowry is usual. In other

communities there may be a "bride price." In some communities, brides may be "captured" or elopements may precede a marriage. It is not unheard-of among hill peoples for parents to arrange an elopement to avoid the expense of a wedding!

EDUCATION

Education is not something to be taken for granted in Nepal. According to UNICEF data, the total adult literacy rate for the period 2000–04 was estimated to be 48.6 percent; for women the figure was just 34.9 percent. Many children do not attend school regularly. Of those enrolled, less than two-thirds complete five years of primary education.

Although the situation is improving, access to education is still heavily dependent on caste, economic status, geographical location, and culture. Education is an aspiration and most middle-class families pay a lot of money to send their children to private schools, where they are expected to study hard. Other children attend local state schools and may be required to contribute to the family income. Not everyone considers it necessary to educate daughters, although scholarships providing girls with free books and uniforms have helped reduce their disadvantage. Most schools are in urban areas. Children in remote areas often have to walk miles to get there.

The academic year begins in the Nepalese month of Baisakh (mid-April), and has three terms. There are two to three weeks' vacation at Dasain and Tihar in October, two weeks' winter vacation in January, and a four-week session break in March/April. The school day is generally from 10:00 a.m. to 4:00 p.m., although some schools in the Terai operate from 6:00 a.m. to 11:00 a.m. during the hottest months of the year.

Kindergartens as we know them do not generally exist. In "nursery" and "kindergarten" classes in private schools, children from the age of three are taught the English and Nepalese alphabets, numbers 1 to 100, and basic English before being permitted to enter Class 1.

Primary education covers Grades 1–5, from the age of six. Lower Secondary (Grades 6–8) and Upper Secondary (Grades 9–10) follow. In Grade 10 pupils sit for the School Leaving Certificate (SLC). Two years' Higher Secondary education known as "Ten plus Two" may follow. These are

semi-specialized (humanities, science, commerce, or education), and qualify pupils for university. Some professional and technical education is available but it is relatively new and restricted to urban areas.

Facilities are generally primitive. Classes of up to one hundred pupils are not unusual in urban areas. Books and uniforms must be bought. The emphasis is on rote learning and theory rather than practical application. Many teachers have only studied up to Class 10 themselves and do not receive any further training.

You will often see signs in Nepal for "English Boarding Schools." These are in fact private day schools in which English is the language of instruction. Many are little more than money-making ventures, but they are successful because the system works for those educated in English. The burgeoning of private schools has improved standards but it has also led to a two-class system that widens the social and economic divide.

Education has been badly damaged by the Maoist insurgency. Many schools have been forced to close down, and both teachers and pupils have been subject to intimidation. It is estimated that in some areas up to a hundred days of schooling per year have been lost because of general strikes or compulsory participation in "political education" sessions required by the Maoists.

UNIVERSITIES

Founded in 1959, Tribhuvan University is the oldest and largest university in Nepal. It comprises institutes of medicine, engineering, science and technology, forestry, social sciences, humanities, management, education, and law, dotted throughout the country. Other universities, all founded in the 1980s and 1990s, are the Mahendra Sanskrit University, Kathmandu University, Pokhara University in the west, Purbanchal University in the east, and the only Buddhist university, Siddhartha. They offer bachelor's and master's degrees, doctorates, and some lower-level proficiency or technical certificates. Due to lack of funding, very little research is conducted.

Few reference works are available in Nepali, so the language of instruction is usually English. Many lecturers have completed master's degrees abroad.

University education is generally the reserve of the elite. In some cases graduates may expect a well-paid placement automatically upon graduation. Graduates have "made it" and do not expect to have to perform menial tasks or physical work again.

Many students belong to the student wings of political parties. The student movements are seen as testing grounds for political parties.

RADIO AND TV

Radio and TV have the edge over print media in a country with such high illiteracy rates and inaccessible terrain. Radios are common even in remote mountain areas. Democracy brought an end to the monopoly of the state-owned Radio Nepal in the mid-1990s. There is now strong competition from FM stations, including pirate stations run by the Maoists.

As almost anywhere else in the world, television

is the most popular form of home entertainment—witness the mushrooming of satellite dishes in the most unlikely locations. The first Nepalese TV channel began broadcasting in 1985, under the motto "Communication for Development." Its mission was to "produce and telecast programs on educational, religious and cultural conservation, to promote national unity, conserve heritage and promote national interest." A private broadcasting sector developed from 1993, and broadcasting via satellite began in 2001, making signals available over much greater areas of the country. Reception is now limited only by the availability of electricity and relay stations.

There are now two state TV channels and six private channels. Many foreign channels are available by satellite. The emphasis is on Hindi movies and Nepalese and Indian soap operas, but news and cultural programs, as well as talk shows, music programs, and documentaries are also shown. Nepal Television and Radio Nepal broadcast some news bulletins in English.

THE PRESS

Newspapers are freely available only in urban areas. Punctual availability can be hampered by weather conditions affecting air deliveries to towns outside the Kathmandu valley.

Gorkhapatra and *Kantipur* are Nepalese-language dailies. The former is published by the government. *Budhabar* is a popular weekly, ideologically associated mainly with the left-wing Communist Party of Nepal (United Marxist-Leninist, not the Maoists—see page 30). *Deshantar* is a weekly publication generally associated with the largest party, the centrist Nepali Congress.

chapter six

TIME OUT

LEISURE

The Nepalese spend the majority of their leisure time with their family. Weekends are short, given the six-day working week everywhere except the Kathmandu valley, and people do not generally go on vacation as we might. They do however make the effort to get home at holiday times. Married women return to their *maiti* (original family) for a break when they can.

You may be invited to join friends on an excursion to a famous religious site or to a local amusement park for a "picnic." It is not sandwiches that are packed up for this (bread not being a constituent of the Nepalese diet), but cooking utensils, kerosene stoves, and everything needed to cook a full-scale *dhal baat*. They may arrange for a car and will aim to arrive early at a designated picnic area, switch on the boom box, and spend the rest of the day cooking, eating, relaxing, possibly dancing, as well as enjoying any attractions there might be. What no one is likely to do voluntarily is to march off into the mountains with a backpack—that is the reserve of tourists and porters.

EATING OUT

Dhal baat, the national dish, is wholesome, tasty, and freshly prepared. High-caste Hindus may avoid meat for religious reasons, and not everyone can afford it, so it is usually accompanied by curried vegetables and

achar (spicy chutney). *Roti* are sometimes served instead of rice. *Kwati*, a soup made of different sprouted beans, is often served at festivals. *Gundruk*, fermented and dried green vegetables, is a specialty in the hills.

Newari food is more diverse, especially when it comes to meat, and water buffalo meat in particular. Not much of the animal is wasted, so as well as steak, soup, or meatballs, you may find tongue, liver, or brains on the menu, all cooked in spicy sauces.

Momos are a sort of Nepalese fast food— steamed dumplings filled with buffalo meat or vegetables and served with a spicy sauce.

If ordering meat, you should be aware that the Nepalese do not section carcasses into the joints and cuts typical in the West. Instead, slices are hacked off and then further hacked into small pieces to be eaten on the bone. Meat often contains bone splinters and gristle. Look out or ask for "boneless" meat.

Outside tourist areas, *dhal baat* is likely to be what is available, although some better restaurants in urban centers may offer a few Indian dishes. If, after a week's trekking, you feel the need for some diversification, restaurants in Kathmandu and Pokhara offer an incredible range of different types of food, from a full English breakfast to Chinese, Italian, Mexican, Tibetan, Japanese, French, or Russian specialties.

When ordering food, remember that things are likely to be cooked very fresh—the chicken may still be flapping around when you place the order. There may well be just one cook producing everything. If everyone orders something different you may sit there for a very long time.

The Nepalese often drink water with their meal. You should only do likewise if you are absolutely certain it is safe to do so. International brands of fizzy drinks are bottled in Nepal and several breweries produce beer.

These are often the safest option. *Rakshi* (distilled from rice), *chang* (Tibetan beer), or *tongba* (a drink made of fermented millet) may also be available. Tea, usually made with milk, is available everywhere. Coffee, although grown in Nepal for export, is generally only available in the tourist areas. As dishes are generally left to drip-dry, you should also ensure plates and glasses are dry before using them.

Wherever you choose to eat out in Nepal, people are friendly and eager to please. If traveling with children you may even find it liberating: where else will a waiter take the time to build paper airplanes with your son, fold lotus flowers out of serviettes for your daughter, or carry your baby around while you eat in peace?

TIPPING

Tipping is common and expected by waiters, cleaners, and luggage porters in restaurants and hotels in tourist areas. Tips constitute a significant proportion of the earnings of porter-guides in the mountains. For cleaners and porters at airports, some loose change is sufficient. In expensive restaurants you should tip up to 10 percent. This is also appropriate for porter-guides. Tipping is not expected in self-service restaurants, nor by taxi and rickshaw drivers.

CROWDS AND LACK OF PRIVACY

"Privacy" is not even a concept in this collective society. The word does not exist in the Nepalese language. The nature of Nepalese life means that much activity is conducted in the open. You can have your hair cut outside, medical treatment may be administered at the pharmacist's counter, a tailor may measure you for new clothes on the street. You may also find yourself trying to make an international telephone call in an open-fronted shop, where noise from the road outside is likely to be a far greater problem than any worries about confidentiality. Protecting what you consider to be "your own space" can be difficult, especially when you are the exotic species! Complete strangers may walk into your house uninvited, their only pretext to see how you live. Similarly, you can expect an audience on any shopping excursion outside the main tourist areas.

Your shopping at local markets will often be as much fun for your audience as it is for you. The fun begins when you try to buy rice. There are numerous different words meaning rice in Nepalese, and a pulses and cereals shop will have various sacks for you to choose from. You might think you are doing well to remember *dhal baat* and ask for "*baat*," but this will just get you a grin—and maybe an invitation to sit down for a plate of cooked rice.

Laughter is the Spice of Life

I caused hilarity in the market one day when I tried to buy a selection of spices—usually sold by the kilogram in Nepal, which was the problem, as I was looking for the sort of quantity you would find in a Western supermarket, which is probably nearer 50g (1.76 oz). I tried telling them we only planned to stay for two years, but that just made them laugh all the more.

You may not always enjoy the constant entourage, but at least you are never likely to feel threatened personally by crowds in Nepal. Nor will you be constantly hassled by persistent beggars.

SHOPPING FOR PLEASURE

It is possible to buy almost anything in Kathmandu. A wide range of imported merchandise is on offer, from beef—not an everyday commodity in a Hindu country—to the latest in digital cameras. Visitors are however most likely to be interested by the country's vast range of different handicrafts, production of which is concentrated in the Kathmandu valley.

Hand-knotted carpets are produced by Tibetans at the refugee camp in Jawalakhel on the edge of Patan, or around the Buddhist stupa at Bodhnath. Here you will also find Tibetan clothing, prayer wheels, and other Buddhist ornaments. Colorful *thangka* paintings, typically depicting the Wheel of Life, are available at Bodhnath, in Bhaktapur, or around Kathmandu's Durbar Square. Their quality and price depend upon the talent and experience of the artist.

Jewelry can be purchased "off the shelf," or created for you with loose gems selected in the shops in Thamel or New Road. You can watch paper products being handmade in Thamel and Bhaktapur. Thimi, between Kathmandu and Bhaktapur, is famous for its papier mâché masks and puppets. Potters display their craft and wares at Potters' Square in Bhaktapur. Highly skilled Newar craftsmen still have workshops in Bhaktapur and Patan, producing traditional wood carvings and engraved copper, brass, and bronze items.

In Thamel you can buy traditional *khukuri* knives, made famous by the Gurkhas, or have your clothes embroidered with a motif of your choice or design. Pashmina wool from the inner coat of Himalayan goats (better known as cashmere) is woven into luxury shawls and other garments on hand looms in the valley and represents one of the country's fastest growing exports.

In most places you will be expected to bargain, but this is all part of the fun. A few words of Nepali may give you a completely different basis for negotiation. Be careful not to insult anyone by pitching your first offer too low. Aim to pay around 20 percent under the asking price.

Very little of what is on sale is old, although unscrupulous traders may try to convince you that you are buying a valuable antique. It is in any case forbidden to export antiques. If something looks old, ask the shop to provide a receipt, and have it approved for export by the Department of Archaeology in Kathmandu, which will issue a permit to wave at customs as you leave.

If you dislike bargaining, or wish to get a feel for what things should cost, there are a few shops in Kathmandu that sell fairly priced goods produced by development projects supporting low-income groups. Ask a taxi driver for "Dhukuti," "Mahaguthi," or "Folk Nepal." The Women's Foundation offers a refuge to displaced women and trains them in such skills as weaving. The pashminas and other woven shawls they produce fund the refuge.

CULTURAL AND SOCIAL LIFE
If it is a riotous nightlife you are after, Nepal is probably not the place to be. You might find bars or nightclubs open late in the tourist areas of

Kathmandu or Lakeside, Pokhara, but you won't meet many Nepalese there. People generally still retire with the sun, even where electricity is available. Outside the Kathmandu valley, any sort of nightlife, including the evening entertaining of guests, is hampered by frequent curfews.

Nor will you find the Western "high culture" of internationally recognized national orchestras, ballet companies, or operas here. The diverse and rich heritage of Nepal instead finds expression in its folklore, epic tales, and religious fables passed on from generation to generation by word of mouth, or enacted in colorful pageants of song and dance, often at temples.

Traditional dance and music are popular and reflect the religious, cultural, and personal experiences of the Nepalese people. They form an integral part of Sanskrit epics, so that many

religious festivals involve dancing at the temple.
People will dance at home, and traditional songs
and dances also form part of any school concert.
Dance performances are often provided for
tourists. Though this on the one hand represents
a commercialization of Nepalese culture and
music, it has also helped preserve folk arts by
providing an income for musicians and dancers.

Conventional theater with its formal stage
settings and props is very much the domain of the
elite and privileged classes. Theater has however
traditionally been used in Hindu and Buddhist
cultures and religious rites for centuries.
Traditional dance-dramas relate the stories of
religious heroes. There are masked performances,
and regionally distinct folk theater performances.
Since the 1980s, various NGOs have successfully
used street theater to advocate democracy, or raise

awareness of social issues such as AIDS, maternal mortality in childbirth, or human rights.

Cinemas are a popular form of entertainment, second only to television. Men and women sit on different sides of the auditorium to watch films. The program tends to be dominated by Bollywood movies, shown in Hindi, occasionally with English subtitles. Hindi is related to Nepalese and widely understood in Nepal.

Nepal does however also boast its own film industry, which began as early as 1951 with a Nepalese-language film produced in India. After the establishment of the Royal Nepal Film Corporation in 1971, the industry mushroomed, reaching a peak in the early nineties. Films are often made with Indian help and actors, and the Bollywood influence is obvious. Most offer their audiences *masaala*, that is, a cocktail of spices—almost always a variation on themes of love and betrayal, with lots of violence and melodramatic music thrown in. Bomb attacks, curfews, and transportation strikes all but stifled the industry during the Maoist insurgency, but production has now resumed.

There are several art galleries in Kathmandu, exhibiting both historical and contemporary works. Religious motifs dominate. Ordinary Nepalese people are confronted with religious art every day in their temples. The Maithili and Tharu peoples of the Terai decorate the adobe walls of their houses with murals, drawing on folklore and

religion as themes.
Development projects
have encouraged the
transfer of these motifs on
to paper as an income-
generating scheme.
Examples can be bought
locally or in Kathmandu.

Pilgrims Bookshop in Thamel, Kathmandu, is a
good starting point for investigating Nepalese
literature. Various folktales, legends, and children's
stories are available in translation (English, plus
some French and German) and show the origins
of many Nepalese beliefs, customs, traditions, and
inhibitions. Some renowned Nepalese writers have
also produced works in English. These include
collections of short stories and essays on current
issues that give invaluable insights into
contemporary Nepalese society.

SPORTS

Nepal is not a nation of sports fanatics, although
cricket is probably the sport that brings it closest.
Plain dwellers will say it is too hot, while those in
the mountains have no need for any further
cardiovascular expansion! Modesty requirements
further restrict women. The results of Asian
sports competitions are however enthusiastically
reported in the press, and events such as the

World Cup draw television spectators despite the country's nonparticipation. Expats living in Kathmandu may have occasion to play football or cricket against other organizations or school groups, and there are elite sports and golf clubs in Kathmandu and Pokhara.

The Nepalese sport of choice around Dasain (October), after the monsoon, when the air is fresh and winds are high, is kite flying. Thousands take to the skies at this time—some as primitive as plastic bags on strings, others far more elaborate. This is more of a competition than you might think, as the object is to drive nearby kites out of the sky. Also at this time of year, huge swings are built from fresh, supple bamboo poles lashed together with rope.

THE GREAT OUTDOORS

The appeal of Nepal for most visitors is of course its unique landscape, which offers some of the finest trekking in the world, the ultimate in mountaineering, some of the planet's most spectacular and arduous mountain biking routes, and the dramatic thrills of white-water rafting down some of the world's deepest, steepest gorges—all sorts of things, in other words, that most Nepalese don't do!

Trekking

Most of Nepal can still only be accessed on foot. Trekking is thus the only way to visit remote communities. The most popular trekking routes are the trek to Everest base camp, those in the Helambu and Langtang valleys north of Kathmandu, and those in the Annapurna region near Pokhara. The advantage of trekking in these regions is that you can expect to find lodges offering food and accommodation at frequent intervals along the way, so that it is quite possible to trek independently, even with children. If you want to trek off the beaten path, the chances are that you will have to be quite self-sufficient.

Lodges on the main routes are simple, generally clean, and inexpensive, although food and drinks become more expensive with increasing altitude (someone has to carry it all up there). Facilities are shared. Staff in lodges usually speak some English, but an English-speaking porter-guide, arranged through your hotel in Pokhara or a reputable agency, can be a worthwhile

investment. They walk with you, recommend lodges, and are happy to fill you in on cultural details or quirks of the mountains as you trek. They will also advise you on how to react to Maoists' requests for "donations." On the main trekking routes permits to enter the National Parks are

required. Permits are also required for trekking in more remote areas.

Mountaineering

Eight out of ten of the world's highest mountains are in Nepal. You can only climb them as part of an official expedition. As a result of the devastation caused by large expeditions felling trees for firewood and abandoning all sorts of mountaineering equipment, the Nepalese government now restricts the number of expeditions and charges fees, which have become an important source of hard currency for the country.

Mountain Biking

Mountain bikes can be rented in Kathmandu. Once you have escaped the traffic, this is one of the best ways to visit out-of-the-way temples, stupas, and villages around the valley. The Tribhuvan Highway from Kathmandu to Hetauda will challenge the fittest with a grueling ascent to 13,123 feet (4,000 m). The reward is an incomparable view of Himalayan peaks from a viewing point at Daman, followed by a dramatic descent through rhododendron forests.

White-water Rafting

Depending on the season, Nepal's rivers rage or meander through lush green valleys and deep gorges, offering rafting for both beginners and the more experienced. The most popular river is the easily accessible Trishuli, which can take you from west of Kathmandu all the way down to Chitwan National Park. You are likely to see more white water and wildlife on other, more remote rivers, however.

Chitwan National Park

No trip to Nepal would be complete without a visit to Chitwan. An elephant safari is an excellent way of exploring the jungle. You may spot wild rhinos, deer, peacocks, and crocodiles. Tigers are more elusive.

chapter seven

TRAVEL, HEALTH, & SAFETY

ARRIVING

Most visitors arriving in Nepal land at the country's only international airport, Kathmandu's Tribhuvan International Airport. There are three main overland routes from India, and one from Tibet.

Drivers must be in possession of an international carnet. They must also leave the country again with their vehicles or face astronomical import duties. Buses operate on all four routes.

The cool polished floors and unhurried lines of Tribhuvan's modern, air-conditioned international terminal may surprise you. They certainly do little to prepare you for what awaits outside! Only traveling passengers are permitted to enter the building, so you won't be hassled by peddlers.

If you are being picked up, you may be met with garlands of flowers or Buddhist shawls—a special honor for "auspicious guests." Independent travelers can best reach the center by taxi. These generally have black license plates and will be waiting outside. The driver may well try to take you to a hotel he knows, so be clear about what you want. For trips from the airport to locations within the beltway there is normally a fixed rate.

When you leave again you should make sure you have enough Nepalese rupees left to pay the international departure tax (US $12–15) at the check-in.

URBAN TRANSPORTATION

When you exit the airport compound on to the beltway, calm gives way to chaos. All of a sudden you will find yourself part of a teeming mass of taxis, cars, buses, trucks, auto-rickshaws, bicycle rickshaws, motorcycles, three-wheeled *tempo* "buses," pedestrians, bicycles, to say nothing of holy cows nonchalantly chewing the cud in the middle of it all.

Traffic is both noisy and filthy, but this probably has more to do with the age and efficiency of the vehicles than with speed. Congestion means that nothing actually moves very fast. The chaos results from volume of traffic and, to Western eyes at least, an apparent lack of adherence to any formal highway code. Officially people drive on the left. Many drivers are not properly trained, licensed, or insured. There are few sidewalks outside Kathmandu.

Private Vehicles

Import taxes even on old cars are prohibitive, so very few Nepalese own a car. The vehicle of choice for middle-class families is a motorbike. Among wealthy families, a motorbike is also a typical wedding present for a son-in-law. There is nothing unusual in seeing a motorcyclist taking his wife to the market, and dropping off a couple of children at school on the way. You may even see a goat riding pillion on the way home for slaughter! Otherwise people use the public transportation that is available.

Taxis

Taxis are largely confined to Kathmandu and Pokhara. Make sure the meter is switched on before you set off, or negotiate a price for your journey in advance. Hiring a taxi for the day is arguably the best way to explore the Kathmandu valley and, particularly if there are a few of you, it is not expensive. If you need a taxi outside the Kathmandu and Pokhara areas, ask around—a local hotel will normally arrange for a car for you.

Thuk-thuks, Rickshaws, and Bicycles

Few towns in Nepal are big enough to warrant city buses. Instead there are *thuk-thuks*. These auto-rickshaws, also known as *tempos*, are spluttering, three-wheeled scooters. The smaller ones carry two or three passengers, tend to be metered, and operate much as taxis do, although they are far less comfortable. The bigger ones are designed for eight to ten people, may well be carrying fifteen, and operate on fixed routes, with each passenger paying a few rupees to the boy hanging on at the back. They can be useful for short distances, but the problem for tourists is often how to recognize where they are going.

Bicycle rickshaws are a common sight in the old part of Kathmandu, and in towns in the Terai. They are slow and bumpy, but can be useful for short distances through crowded, narrow streets, or if you don't want to walk in the dusty heat. It is

as well to find out what remuneration is expected before you set off; you will be charged more in tourist areas.

Bicycles can be an ideal way of getting around small towns. Smog and chaotic traffic are hazards in Kathmandu.

GETTING AROUND THE COUNTRY

Any long-distance journey in Nepal is likely to be something of an adventure. Distances are not huge, but delays are frequent and progress slow. However, some of the most dramatic scenery in the world goes a long way toward compensating for any discomfort, and you will rarely make a journey without collecting an enduring memory of some cameo of Nepalese life.

With just one 30-mile (48-km) stretch of

railway from Janakpur in the Terai to Jaynagar in India, the majority of travelers stick to a standard itinerary of destinations on roads in the middle of the country. The road network is one of the least developed in the world. Although expanding

gradually, it is still largely limited to the busy Mahendra Highway that runs the length of Nepal's southern border, and the Prithvi Highway, which runs west from Kathmandu along the Trishuli River to Mugling and on to Pokhara. A small section of this highway branches south at Mugling to join the Mahendra Highway at Narayanghat.

The first road to connect Kathmandu with the outside world was the Tribhuvan Highway, built by the Indian government in the 1950s. This considerable feat of engineering winds directly south over the mountains from the Prithvi Highway at Naubise to Hetauda, and on to the Indian border at Birgunj. The tortuous 67 miles (107 m) from Naubise to Hetauda are worth it for the views, but take six to eight hours by car. Accordingly, most traffic traveling to and from Kathmandu now uses the Prithvi Highway via Narayanghat.

Only the Mahendra Highway is consistently wide enough for buses to pass without slowing down. On narrow stretches of road smaller vehicles give way to larger ones for reasons of self-preservation! Maintenance of the highways is irregular and, especially during and just after the monsoon, landslides frequently render roads impassable, causing huge delays. The Tribhuvan Highway may also be closed in winter due to snow.

Buses

Bus stations are chaotic, with vendors milling around offering bottled water and snacks to eat on your journey. Destinations are not always written in English, so you may have to ask for help. Buses are well used, so it is better to buy your ticket a day in advance. If staying in Kathmandu or Pokhara, you can ask your hotel to arrange for tickets.

Private and state bus companies operate along all paved roads in Nepal. Buses are cheap. They are also uncomfortable, crowded, noisy, dirty, slow, and prone to breakdown and overheating. They may

have suicidally high centers of gravity due to the number of passengers, goats, suitcases, and sofas perched on the roof. As drivers sometimes also give the impression that they are relying a little too much on *karma*, you should be prepared for a thrilling ride. Reports of buses leaving the road to plunge into a gorge are not infrequent.

Journeys are delayed further by multiple police and army checks that entail everyone alighting to walk through a checkpoint (foreigners sometimes excepted), not to mention various tea and *dhal baat* stops at the driver's discretion.

If you are traveling between Kathmandu, Pokhara and Chitwan, Greenline tourist buses, though slightly more expensive, are a better bet. They are cleaner and better maintained, tend to be driven more carefully, and stop only at Greenline stations, where facilities are clean and a *dhal baat* buffet is included in the price of your ticket. Tourist buses have the additional advantage of sometimes being waved through police checks.

Car and Bike Rental

It is not generally possible to rent a car and drive it yourself in Nepal. Instead, you hire one with a driver. This has advantages. A driver will know where to find gas, and where he can leave the car. He is also used to the peculiarities of the Nepalese highways and of his often poorly maintained vehicle. And if the worst comes to the worst and you do have an accident, it could save you a lot of hassle. If you arrange for a driver outside Kathmandu to take you to the capital, you should be aware that he is only permitted to take you as far as the beltway ("the ringroad"). City taxis have exclusive licenses for the area within the beltway.

Motorbikes can be hired in Kathmandu and are a versatile way of seeing the country: they can usually be pushed around craters in the road, and if the road disappears, you can always take to the riverbed! Beware of the drops in temperature that come with altitude and be sure to pack scarf and gloves.

Flying

Aircraft are a crucial component of Nepal's transport infrastructure, especially in the far west region, where they are used to airlift food supplies in winter. Some airstrips are two or more days' walk from the nearest road. Nepal Airlines (formerly Royal Nepal Airlines) and several private airlines operate small propeller aircraft between various towns. Most flights start or end in Kathmandu.

In clear conditions a domestic flight can be a

fascinating experience in itself, and it certainly saves a lot of time. Flights are however often disrupted by fog or other poor weather conditions. Domestic airports are fairly basic, so make sure you have something to eat and drink with you in case your flight is delayed.

Visitors are expected to pay for flights in hard currency and pay significantly more than residents. A porter may carry your luggage to or from your taxi or bus but will expect a small tip.

WHERE TO STAY

In the Kathmandu valley, Pokhara, and around Chitwan National Park you will find all grades of accommodation, from basic budget hostels to five-star hotels with swimming pools. Tourist numbers have been down because of the Maoist troubles, so competition for your business is quite fierce. If traveling independently you can often negotiate a good price on the spot for a pleasant room including a private bathroom, hot water, and breakfast. People will go out of their way to be helpful and arrange for anything else you need.

In bigger towns in the Terai a range of standards of accommodation may be available, with little choice at the top end. Bear in mind when looking for accommodation here that it can get very hot, and that mosquitoes can be a problem. Look for rooms with fans and mosquito nets as a minimum.

Accommodation in lodges on major trekking routes is plentiful, simple, and adequate. Here it is advisable to take your own sleeping bag.

Away from the major tourist haunts and urban centers, accommodation is likely to be primitive. In the Terai especially it may be quite dirty. The same applies to many hotel kitchens.

It can be arranged to stay with Nepalese families. The accommodation is not likely to be luxurious, but you will be warmly received and the experience will give you a fascinating insight into the Nepalese way of life, routines, and customs.

HEALTH AND SAFETY

There are no obligatory vaccinations for a visit to Nepal, but you should ensure all basic vaccinations are up to date, and check current recommendations for other appropriate vaccinations with your embassy or the Ciwec Clinic Travel Medicine Center in Kathmandu before you travel. There are incidences of both Japanese encephalitis and malaria in Nepal. Whether you need vaccinations or prophylactic medication will depend on where you will be spending time. Rabies vaccinations are a consideration if traveling to remote areas because of the time needed to get back to civilization in

 the event of being bitten. It may also be necessary to take precautions against hepatitis, typhoid, and meningitis. Tuberculosis is endemic in Nepal, but the risk to travelers is low unless you are going to spend lots of time with lots of people in enclosed places.

For longer stays a good basic health care manual, such as *Where There Is No Doctor—A Village Health Care Handbook* by David Werner, is recommended, not only for your personal requirements, but because you may also be asked for advice. It can be helpful to talk to locals, as they sometimes recognize symptoms you may not have encountered before.

Although there are some good clinics in Kathmandu, Pokhara, and one or two places lucky enough to have mission hospitals, health facilities in most other locations are poor or nonexistent. Medical treatment at Western travelers' clinics is expensive. Comprehensive travel and health insurance is essential.

Many medicines are readily available for purchase at pharmacies—with or without prescriptions, and in many cases much cheaper than they would be in the West. Especially in mountain regions, it is better to have a supply of antiseptics and antibiotics with you than to rely on finding them. You will also be removing them from the very scanty stocks of remote mountain outposts.

If you do have to seek help, doctors will speak English. Other staff may not. In the event of admission to hospital, it is as well to know that relatives and friends are normally expected to bring in all food and be on hand to run errands, such as going to the hospital pharmacy to purchase any medicines, anesthetics, or other equipment that may be needed.

Water and Dairy Products

If accidents are the biggest single risk to the lives of visitors to Nepal, the biggest single potential health risk is undoubtedly the water. In many places sewers are open. Sewage and water pipes often leak and may be one above the other. You can catch amoebic dysentery, typhoid, diarrhea, hepatitis, bacterial infections, worms, and other parasites, so never drink from a tap, accept water to drink if you are not certain it has been both boiled and filtered, eat fruit you have not peeled or washed yourself in safe water, brush your teeth with the water, or sing in the shower—it's far better to keep your mouth shut! Rivers are polluted with refuse—floating, sunk, swimming or, in the case of the cadavers, bouncing along bloated.

Milk and other dairy products may also be a problem. Milk should be boiled even if the bag does say "pasteurized." Bhaktapur is famous for its delicious yogurt, but you should always scrape the top off, as it is left to set in open bowls in the sun, often at the roadside.

NATURAL HAZARDS
Altitude
Altitude sickness can and does kill. To avoid it, ascend slowly and give yourself plenty of time to acclimatize. If symptoms of nausea, tiredness, and severe headaches persist, you should return to a lower altitude and seek medical advice.

Don't stand on the valley side of a path to let a mule train pass!

Flooding and Landslides

Road conditions are poor at the best of times in Nepal, but the arrival of the monsoon can turn trickling streams into raging torrents capable of tearing away bridges and transporting rocks the size of houses miles downstream. Flooding and frequent landslides are the result, rendering many roads impassable and cutting off remote regions.

Earthquakes

Earth tremors are common in this region and may also cause landslides and/or avalanches. The last major earthquake to hit the country was in 1934, when it is believed that twenty thousand people were killed. Experts believe that another major earthquake is now overdue. "Earthquake kits" are available in some tourist shops. They include bottled water, canned food, and a spade. Some hotels in Kathmandu provide information on how to behave in the event of an earthquake—it is as well to read it.

CRIME

As in any big city across the world, you should be wary of pickpockets in the bustle of Kathmandu. The country no doubt also has its share of unscrupulous swindlers plying dubious wares. Crime levels in Nepal are however relatively low. With luck, nothing worse will happen to you than a half-eaten biscuit being swiped from your hand by a monkey in an unguarded moment at Swayambunath!

There have been reports of trekkers being robbed, but this is not common. As anywhere, you should stick to the main routes. Do not trek alone.

As far as the Maoist insurgents are concerned, they are as aware as any other political group of the significance of development aid, and have so far done everything in their power to avoid involving foreigners in violence. There have been occasional reports of tourists being beaten for having refused to "make a donation," but this is unusual, and most trekkers seem to see a furtive meeting with the Maoists early in the morning on the way up Poon Hill as part of the experience. The Maoists will voluntarily issue a souvenir receipt!

POLITICAL HAZARDS

Despite the peace agreement signed on November 21, 2006, between the Maoists and the government, the political situation in Nepal remains volatile. Street demonstrations, rallies, disturbances, and roadblocks continue throughout the country as political groups try to gain influence. Generally it is advisable to stay away from anything that looks like an organized gathering.

Violence has not so far been directed at foreign visitors. The situation does however affect your free passage across country, as frequent *bandhs* (general strikes), sometimes lasting several days, really do shut everything down. It may be necessary to stockpile food in advance of longer strikes, although small shops often reopen surreptitiously on the second or third day, allowing customers in through a back door.

Bandhs may be regional or nationwide. Sometimes there is advance warning, but you should be aware that they can be called at short notice, and you are stranded or restricted to pedal power until they end. It is thus advisable to plan your return to Kathmandu several days before a flight out of the country. There is an upside to these general strikes: they allow you to explore the Kathmandu valley by bike without risking either your neck or your lungs.

DON'T MISS
A Walk Through Old Kathmandu
Take a walk through the teeming lanes between Durbar Square and Thamel and allow your senses to be assaulted by the vibrant colors of women's saris, gaudy shop fronts, and powder-smeared shrines, the scents of incense and spices, and the cacophony of horns, bells, and tradesmen's calls.

Bhaktapur
Wander through the brick-paved alleys of this perfectly preserved medieval city, with its temples,

pagoda roofs, and elaborate carvings. Bhaktapur is cleaner than Kathmandu and traffic is largely banned from its center.

Bodhnath
Circumambulate this oasis of calm in the bustle of Kathmandu.

Pashupatinath
The goal of countless pilgrims and *sadhus*, this is Hinduism's most important religious site in Nepal.

Swayambunath
Climb the steps to this Buddhist stupa in the evening for a view over the entire Kathmandu valley.

Seeing the Mountain Skyline at Dawn
To be next to the roof of the world and not take a look at the mountain setting as the curtains rise

would be a serious omission. Watch an unforgettable
sunrise from Nagarkot, Dhulikhel, or Daman.

A Trek
Discover idyllic villages, perfectly tended terraces,
and the stark beauty of the mountains.

Chitwan
Don't miss an elephant safari in Chitwan National
Park—the ideal way to go tiger- and rhino-spotting.

Festivals
Participate in any festival you happen to be there for
(see Chapter 3).

chapter eight

BUSINESS BRIEFING

THE BUSINESS ENVIRONMENT

Since democratization in 1991, the Nepalese economy has been liberalized. Although red tape and corruption can still be a problem, licensing requirements have been simplified, company and commercial legislation revised, and a new tax system introduced. Tariffs have been reduced on some commodities, notably industrial raw materials. Customs duties are relatively low except for a few luxury items (vehicles: 130 percent!). Industrial machinery can be imported at a special rate of just 2.5 percent.

A number of banks and financial companies have come to Nepal as a result of liberalization and provide commercial and financial services for businesses. The Nepalese rupee is fully convertible on current accounts for goods and services.

The obstacles to economic development remain considerable, however. They begin with a lack of natural resources, and a topography that renders most of the country inaccessible except on foot. Even the one reliable road route from India to Kathmandu is subject to frequent blockages during periods of unrest, general strikes, or as a result of landslides during the monsoon. Nepal is landlocked, and thus dependent on India allowing transport of goods to the sea in Kolkata, approximately 715 miles (1,150 km) from the Nepal–India border. Other problems are a poorly educated population, fatalism, overdependence on foreign aid, a feudal system and lack of meritocracy, political stagnation and infighting, ethnic and religious discord, a weak civil society, and corruption. The situation has been exacerbated by the devastation and insecurity caused by the insurgency.

You are not likely to find yourself dealing with huge multinationals or financial asset corporations in Nepal. Seventy-five percent of the population is still engaged in agriculture, and the country's limited manufacturing sector, mainly located in the Kathmandu valley and the Terai, is largely occupied with processing agricultural resources. Most businesses are small, family-run concerns. Foreign investors include Unilever, Coca-Cola, Standard Chartered, and Hyatt (hotels). Most investors are, however, individuals. The main areas for investment are hydropower, tourism,

telecommunications, civil aviation, and
information technology. There are
opportunities in renewable energy
technology, pharmaceuticals,
security equipment and services,
and education (especially
vocational qualifications and IT).

Disruption
As mentioned above, politically motivated *bandhs*
(general strikes) regularly bring whole areas of the
country to a halt. Businesses may be subject to
attack if they continue to operate during *bandhs*,
and employees may be prevented from reaching
work by the lack of any means of road transport.

BUSINESS CULTURE
Personal relationships are the key to business
deals in Nepal. Your initial contact may well be
made through business associates or common
acquaintances. As nothing much gets done
without the help of influential contacts, it is
therefore important to establish personal
connections with as many people as possible.

Initially relations may be very formal.
Thereafter it is sincerity, cordiality, and a personal
approach that will build up the necessary level of
mutual respect and trust. A business relationship

will rarely be built up over the phone—the Nepalese want to know exactly who they are dealing with. Socializing will thus play a role.

Entertaining may be one way of getting yourself an audience, although some high-caste Hindus may not wish to visit restaurants for reasons of purity (they cannot eat food prepared by lower-caste people). You may be invited to people's homes. Dinner will be seen as an opportunity to continue business discussions, as well as to get to know you. This takes time, and you should not hurry it (see pages 87–8).

Fatalism may lead to an attitude to business that can on occasion be downright lackadaisical. Success is good *karma*, failure bad *karma*. The belief in cycles means that opportunities missed this time may well come round again. You may also find a reliance on superstition rather than rational planning: astrology may be used to determine "auspicious days" for meetings or the conclusion of a contract.

Another key attitude that comes across in business relations is the Nepalese respect for their elders. Older participants in meetings will be treated with politeness and deference. It is also reflected in forms of address. It is polite to say *Namascar* instead of *Namaste* to an older person. If addressing people by name, you should add the *-jee* suffix as a mark of respect.

Status and Hierarchy

Most businesses in Nepal are hierarchical and patriarchal. Even mundane decisions may have to go through several levels, and ultimately, it is the patriarch who decides. This can make for a very slow decision-making process. The *hakim*'s (boss's) word is law. There is no formal review or consultation process. Staff will respect his authority unless it is perceived to be unjust. Having a certain status means getting other people to do things for you as far as possible, and keeping your own hands clean.

Connections

You could say nepotism is rife in Nepal, but the Nepalese don't see it that way. For them it is the familial duty of those in high positions to provide jobs for their associates. Name, caste, and political affiliation all play a role in whether someone is given employment. This is changing slowly with increasing levels of education, but family contacts can still be extremely important. Good relationships with clients or partners will open up new partnerships through their family ties and *aphno manche* connections.

Business Dress

The Nepalese dress formally in office situations. For business meetings you should always err on the side of formality and conservatism. Suits are the norm. Shorts are unacceptable, nor should you wear jeans. You may dispense with the tie in most situations, but a smart shirt with a collar is essential. Short sleeves are generally acceptable. Nepalese businessmen often wear Western dress, whereas women wear traditional saris or a *kurta suruval*. Western women should dress smartly and modestly. Short skirts should be avoided, and shoulders covered.

Women in Business

Greater access to education means that there are increasing numbers of economically active women in Nepal. This is slowly improving their status as they contribute to the family income. Nepalese society is however quite chauvinist by Western standards, and men used to deferential women may be uncomfortable dealing with forthright Western women in positions of authority. It is, however, acceptable for women to meet men in public places.

Social attitudes may force women to give up work upon marriage (they need their husband's permission to work), they may be obliged to bring their baby to work with them (leaving it in a bundle on the floor somewhere while they work), and they may be expected to disappear from the workplace "to cook for a visiting brother-in-law."

There are businesses run by women, and various development projects aim to empower women. Earnings and increased status are liberating and many women are highly motivated.

Business Hours

Office hours in the Kathmandu valley are generally 9:00 a.m. until 5:00 p.m. (9:00 a.m. to 4:00 p.m. in winter), Monday to Friday. Outside the valley people work a six-day week, with Saturday as the only day of rest. Here offices open at 10:00 a.m. Shops are open much longer.

MEETINGS

Making Appointments

It is probably best to make appointments by telephone, especially when meeting for the first time, although e-mail is increasingly used. Make appointments well in advance and, especially outside the capital, allow for Nepalese road conditions to give yourself time to get to the venue punctually. Be aware of Nepalese eating habits, too: an appointment before 10:00 a.m. may not be convenient.

As decisions are generally made at the top, it is advisable to make your approach at this level. In internationally active organizations, secretaries will probably speak some English. It may be a good idea to prepare some phrases in Nepali. Exchanging courtesies with staff will dispose them positively toward you and increase your chances of being passed on to the boss. Alternatively, ask a Nepali speaker to be on hand to help.

At the Meeting
Punctuality is important, although you should not be surprised if you are kept waiting. It may also take a while to get down to

business. First meetings are likely to entail a combination of ceremony and cordiality. Wait to be invited to take a seat. For an initial visit this will probably be on a sofa in a reception room or the boss's office. Do not however be surprised if invited to sit down on a cushion on the floor—this is the traditional way. You will probably be offered tea, which will be brought by a *Didi*, quite likely summoned by a bell. Time at the beginning is given to small talk.

When you walk into a room, you should greet everyone with a *Namaste*. Whether you shake hands with other participants in the meeting will depend on how many of them there are, and who they are. The greater the degree of exposure to Western influence, the more likely people are to expect to shake hands. It is not always appropriate to shake hands with women, and if you are talking to the representatives of rural communities, it will not be expected either. It is probably just as well to wait and see if you are offered a hand. *Namaste* should be answered with *Namaste*.

This is a very verbal culture: there may be an official agenda for the meeting, and there may be a scribe producing minutes, but the emphasis is not on paperwork. Staff memos are not typical. Decisions are pronounced verbally. People sit down together and solve problems by talking.

In urban areas English is widely spoken and understood, but discussions in Nepali may occur between Nepalese within a meeting. Understanding Nepalese English can present a problem, and you may need to ask people politely to repeat themselves. In rural areas you will need an interpreter. Be aware, however, that interpreters may only translate what they *think* you want to hear. The local management representative of a charity, for example, may exaggerate the woes of someone who stands to benefit from a donation, or the potential benefit of that donation. Try to engage an independent translator. Students are often delighted to assist.

Business cards printed in English are likely to be exchanged at the end of meetings. The Nepalese set great store by academic titles and qualifications. These are listed on business cards and it will do no harm to admire them.

Presentations

Common perceptions of what makes a good presentation apply in Nepal, too: it should be succinct, with effective use of visuals. Speak slowly and clearly, and conclude with a summary of the main points to provide a basis for discussion. A professional presentation with graphics and special effects will impress, but the Nepalese also like detailed facts and figures. Both erudition and eloquence are highly valued (they like to use flowery language) and will bring you respect: it is important that you show your education, know-how, and experience. They need to see that your business proposal is serious, that it relates to them, and that you can back it up with strong financial and/or staffing support. They do not take kindly to being dictated to, so make sure you present your proposal as one of partnership, with advantages for both sides. Expect questions and consider suggestions. They will also want to discuss things exhaustively before coming to a decision.

NEGOTIATIONS

Haggling over price is a way of life in Nepal, so expect potential business partners to drive a hard bargain. Do not insult them by offering a price too obviously low. They will expect a compromise solution at the end of negotiations and so should you. On the one hand, your counterparts will be looking for the best deal available. On the other, they may be thinking that the opportunity will come up again: *karma*. This can lead to apathy.

Negotiations sometimes involve many people, and can be protracted. The process is not helped by the fact that the Nepalese may not say exactly what they are thinking. This is because they do not want to offend you or appear ungracious as hosts, and is all about maintaining face. An evasive answer may mean "no." "I'll try" may also mean "but I've no intention of succeeding." Such responses are an attempt to be polite.

If people have to admit they have not understood something, they lose face. This will have consequences: it is essential to give exact information and to make clear what it is you need from them. Refrain from criticizing or correcting colleagues, clients, or potential business partners in the presence of others, and beware of patronizing or appearing arrogant. Emphasize common aims and rely on good relationships to make things possible. The situation can become fraught if things are not settled, but confrontation may humiliate and ultimately alienate people. They will need time to discuss the options, to air their views, and to come to a conclusion. Take time yourself, and do not try to rush those you are negotiating with into a decision.

CONTRACTS

Company and commercial law in Nepal is based on English law. Contracts cover all aspects of a business agreement and are written up by a lawyer. They may be in English or Nepali. They should be formulated in formal, eloquent language and include lots of detail, although you should be prepared for requests for modification.

Successful negotiations may well culminate in a written contract, but you would be ill-advised to rely on one. Oral agreements are very important in Nepal. Contracts may be viewed as provisional declarations of intent, but subject to modification. Quality assurance is not established in Nepal, so that the quality of goods delivered may not match that specified in the contract. Time is neither money nor an issue, so it may be difficult or counterproductive to enforce strict deadlines.

If a conflict of interests does arise, avoid litigation. According to the NGO Transparency International, the police and judiciary are among the most corrupt sectors in Nepal. Basic legal procedures are neither quick nor straightforward.

Regular communication and visits are more effective. Politeness, respect, and praise are important. A trusted person based locally should be identified as soon as possible to deal with things. Many investors appoint one agent for the whole country and maintain central offices in Kathmandu. It is difficult to vet distributors in the absence of a local credit rating company—the financial details they provide cannot easily be substantiated. Here again, relationship-building is crucial. It is essential to see their operations firsthand. Developing contacts with Nepalese banks and leading businessmen can help.

BUREAUCRACY AND *BAKSHEESH*

Theoretically, Nepal's government is open to foreign direct investment. In practice, the government's own bureaucracy may hinder investment through delays and inefficiency. There are often complaints from foreign investors about complex and opaque government procedures, as well as encounters with officials whose attitudes can be more antagonistic than obliging, at least until *baksheesh* comes into play. Originally indicating a gift, this Persian word has mutated to mean bribe—a payment to expedite service. This greasing of the wheels has its historical background in the *jagir* culture (see Chapter 2).

The fact that civil servants are rotated in their positions every two years also tends to slow the wheels, as they are barely there long enough to "learn the ropes." Decisions may be changed retrospectively, forgotten, or not honored. There are frequent allegations of corruption by officials in the distribution and extension of permits and approvals, the procurement of goods and services, and the awarding of contracts.

Even dealing with basic travel documents can require regular, time-consuming attention. It may be easiest to delegate the responsibility for cutting through red tape to a Nepalese associate.

Favors

There may be corruption involved in dealings with government offices, but day-to-day business is not overtly corrupt. What may sometimes seem to Westerners to be corruption is the by-product of a hierarchical, patriarchal society that leads to a reliance on the *aphno manche* system of reciprocal favors—which Nepalis do not regard as corrupt. Favors are a way of maintaining useful contacts in business or of dealing with bureaucracy. Such contacts may later be called upon for assistance.

EMPLOYMENT FOR FOREIGNERS

Unless you are posted to Nepal by a development organization or work for an international NGO, there are few opportunities for formal employment. Foreign technical personnel may be employed, subject to the approval of the Department of Labor. Travelers on tourist visas are not permitted to work for any organization, whether paid or voluntary. Business visas are issued to foreign investors or their representatives. Residential visas are only issued to individuals of international renown or who make a special contribution to the country. Foreigners wishing to engage in business in Nepal must register under the Company Act of 1997.

chapter nine

COMMUNICATING

Nepali is the official language of Nepal and Sikkim, and is also spoken in other parts of northern India, in Bhutan, and in Burma. It is an Indo-Aryan language, closely related to Hindi and Sanskrit, and commonly written in Devanagari script. It is, however, just one of more than ninety languages spoken in Nepal, and the mother tongue of only

47.8 percent of the population. Regionally other languages dominate. Maithili and Bhojpuri are Indo-Aryan languages spoken in the Terai, Newar is common in the Kathmandu valley and central mid-hills, and other Tibeto-Burmese languages are spoken in the north. In these areas, Nepali may be very much a second language.

SPEAKING NEPALI
It is well worth learning some Nepali. It enables you to interact at a different level and with a wider variety of people, giving you a far greater insight

into Nepalese culture. It also gives Nepalese people much pleasure to hear you try!

Nepali is a phonetic, syllabic language, not tonal, and therefore easier to learn than many other Asian languages. It has a simple subject-object-verb structure, postpositions rather than prepositions, and a large number of pronouns that depend on gender, number, and the status of the person in question. Foreigners usually get away with the universally respectful form *tapai* for "you." Colloquial Nepali also has two simplified, nonconjugated verb forms, one for present/future and one for past tenses, which makes life a lot easier.

Many English words have been assimilated, usually to describe things not common in Nepali culture, such as a "*taybull*." Nepalese English can be difficult to understand, however, even when spoken by educated people. Their understanding of colloquial English may also be limited.

The Nepalese love eloquence and use flowery language, which can lead to "round about" ways of saying things. They also like to flatter their audience, using expressions such as "honorable gentlemen" or "esteemed guests."

FACE-TO-FACE

After *Namaste!*, conversations usually move on to a "How are you?" Once you know people, you are expected to show interest in their families.

What is missing in Nepalese are "please" and "thank you." There is a word for the latter, but you will probably only hear other foreigners using it. For the Nepalese, it is natural that people you know should help or give you things—they do not need to be thanked for it. No offense is intended if someone fails to thank you. Rather, it is a sign of trust and friendship. Instead of "please," Nepalese use a polite form of the imperative (*Bill dinus* = Give me the bill). A direct translation may seem rude, but this isn't intended. No one will be be offended if you use *Dhanyabat* (thank you), but it will mark you as a foreigner.

Another characteristic is the use of titles such as *Dai* (older brother), *Bahini* (younger sister), or *Buwa* (father) as polite ways of addressing people who are not in fact relatives. These indicate respect and reflect age or respective status.

The Nepalese do not have difficulty making eye contact with people they consider to be equals. Subordinates do not generally raise their eyes. Men may not expect direct eye contact from women.

BODY LANGUAGE
Body language in Nepal is no less likely to require translation than the spoken language.

A gesture you will often see is a curious sideways rocking of the head. This indicates "OK"/ "Maybe," or a fairly noncommittal "Yes."

The Nepalese beckon with their palms downward. They count with their thumbs on the joints of their fingers—so three on each of four fingers.

If someone throws their hands into the air, as if turning a dial clockwise with the right hand, and counterclockwise with the left, they mean "What do you mean?" or "What's the problem?"

It is not unusual to see men holding hands. This is a mark of platonic friendship only. Men and women do not touch in public.

The feet and shoes are considered to be unclean. Always take your shoes off before you enter someone's house, and be careful never to point the soles of your feet at anyone, as this would be degrading.

The head is traditionally sacred, so you should never touch or pat even a child on the head. It is also extremely disrespectful to step over or pass anyone from above. This is why Nepalese people will wait for you to come down a staircase before going up themselves.

CENSORSHIP

According to Reporters without Borders, Nepal accounted for half of all censorship reports around the globe in the year 2005. Freedom of the press has suffered considerably as a result of civil conflict, with journalists being attacked and intimidated by both sides. Under the state of emergency invoked by King Gyanendra in 2005, all independent media were effectively silenced. In May 2006 the government eased restrictions on the press, but reporters have since been subject to intimidation in new ethnic unrest in the south.

Television has not been exempt. State television channels have developed into government mouthpieces, and licensing procedures for private channels are subject to political influence.

ENGLISH-LANGUAGE PUBLICATIONS

The Kathmandu Post and *The Himalayan Times* are daily English-language newspapers that include some international news. *The Rising Nepal* is an English-language government paper. More detailed analysis of national and international events can be found in the weekly *Nepali Times.*

An organization called Expatriate Community Services (www.ecs.com.np) offers language courses and produces a glossy monthly, *Your Guide To Living in Nepal,* aimed at the expatriate community in Kathmandu. It covers lifestyle, culture, and business in Nepal, and includes features by Nepalese writers and expatriates, as well as a calendar of upcoming events.

International publications, including *Time, Newsweek, The Economist, L'Express, Der Spiegel, Die Zeit,* and *El País* are on sale at Pilgrims Bookshop in Kathmandu.

POSTAL SERVICES

Outbound mail from Nepal is reasonably reliable from Kathmandu or Pokhara. "Snail mail" between towns within Nepal can be slower than sending things internationally, although it does seem to work eventually. Poste restante (general delivery) services are available only in Kathmandu. The main post office in Kathmandu is on Kantipath, near the stadium and New Road. You can buy stamps and hand in letters for posting at Pilgrims Bookshops in Kathmandu and Pokhara.

A faster option is a courier service. This is more expensive than the post but generally reliable and efficient. Couriers are of course as susceptible as any other road user to disruption caused by the weather, landslides, or strikes. You generally need to pick things up from a designated office in the town, signing for anything you receive.

USING THE TELEPHONE

Only the wealthy have telephones at home, and not all of these can make international calls. It is possible to phone abroad and send faxes from telecommunications shops at the market. If you are calling from outside the Kathmandu valley, it can be difficult to get through. This is because all lines out of the country go via Kathmandu.

Nepalis generally have an abrupt telephone manner. They do not say their name, but launch straight into conversation. They're equally abrupt in putting the phone down—usually as soon as they fail to understand you or realize they do not know who you are. This can be very off-putting.

The Internet
There are now Internet cafés in most towns, but connections may not be as fast or reliable as you are used to, especially outside Kathmandu.

CONCLUSION
King Prithvi Narayan Shah, who unified Nepal, described his country as "a flower garden of four *varnas* (castes) and thirty-six *jats* (communities)." This positive image captures the beauty and also the diversity of Nepal. Its incongruities and contrasts will inevitably surprise you. So too, despite the political uncertainty, will its harmony.

Whatever the reason for your visit, a knowledge of Nepalese culture will enhance the experience and give you realistic expectations. Once you get to know the Nepalese, their friendliness, stoicism, warmth, and hospitality will leave a lasting impression, so that when it comes to saying good-bye, the Nepali way will seem the most appropriate: *"Pheri bhetaula!"*—"We'll meet again."

Further Reading

Bista, Dor Bahadur. *Fatalism and Development: Nepal's Struggle for Modernization*. Hyderabad: Orient Longman Pty Limited, 1999.

Chaulagain, Luna (translated by Ganesh Chaulagain and Phil Grayston). *Himalayan Folk Tales*. Nepal: locally published in 2001 and available at Pilgrims Bookshop.

Dixit, Kanak Mani and Ramachandaran, Shastri. *State of Nepal*. Lalitpur, Nepal: Himal Books, 2002.

Finlay, Hugh. *Lonely Planet Nepal*. V**ictoria,** Australia: Lonely Planet Publications Pty Ltd, 2001.

Hutt, Michael and Subedi, Abhi. *Teach Yourself Nepali*. London: Hodder & Stoughton, 1999.

Krakauer, Jon. *Into Thin Air*. London: Pan Books, 1998.

Upadhyay, Samrat. *Arresting God in Kathmandu*. Kolkata: Rupa & Co, 2003.

Werner, David. *Where There Is No Doctor—A Village Health Care Handbook*. London: Macmillan Education, 1993.

Useful Web Sites

www.ecs.com.np
www.nepal.com
www.nepalmountainnews.com
www.nepalnews.com
www.visitnepal.com

Index